P9-BBN-816

Zach,

Keep sharing
Jesus!

Zach,
Keep shavin'!
Tsss!

DARE 2 SHARE

GREG STIER

Tyndale House Publishers, Inc.
Carol Stream, Illinois

Dare 2 Share
Copyright © 2006 by Dare 2 Share Ministries, Inc.
All rights reserved. International copyright secured.

A Focus on the Family book published by
Tyndale House Publishers, Carol Stream, Illinois 60188

TYNDALE and Tyndale's quill logo are registered trademarks of Tyndale House
Publishers, Inc.

The GOSPEL Journey is a trademark of Dare 2 Share Ministries.

All Scripture quotations, unless otherwise indicated, are taken from the *Holy Bible, New
International Version*®. NIV®. Copyright © 1973, 1978, 1984 by International Bible
Society. Used by permission of Zondervan Publishing House. All rights reserved. If bold
appears within a quoted verse, the emphasis was added by the author.

People's names and certain details of their stories have been changed to protect the
privacy of the individuals involved.

No part of this publication may be reproduced, stored in a retrieval system, or transmit-
ted in any form or by any means—electronic, mechanical, photocopy, recording, or
otherwise—without prior permission of Focus on the Family.

Editor: Marianne Hering
Cover design: Jessie McGrath
Character photos in chapters 24–37: Steve Stanton
Author portrait photographer: Wayne Armstrong

Library of Congress Cataloging-in-Publication Data
Stier, Greg.
  Dare 2 share : a field guide to sharing your faith with anyone, anytime, anywhere!/
by Greg Stier.
     p. cm.
ISBN-13: 978-1-58997-370-1
ISBN-10: 1-58997-370-4
  1. Evangelistic work. 2. Witness bearing (Christianity) 3. Apologetics. I. Title: Dare
to share. II. Title.
  BV3790.S84 2006
  248'.5—dc22

                                  2006004270

Printed in the United States of America
        4 5 6 7 8 9 / 12 11 10 09 08 07

*To Jeremy, the little boy who melts my heart
and makes me laugh, may you grow in the love of Jesus
and have a passion to tell everyone about Him.*

TABLE OF CONTENTS

Part Three: Your Guide to Sharing Your Faith with Anyone

ACKNOWLEDGMENTS

I thank God for the help that I received on this project from Lane Palmer and Jane Dratz. Lane and Jane are full-time writers and researchers at Dare 2 Share Ministries who are excellent at what they do.

Lane, thanks for the hard work you put into part 3 of this book. Your research was excellent and your witty, sometimes sarcastic, and always insightful comments make this section especially powerful and practical.

Jane, thanks for your honest input into my writing. You have made me a better writer by pushing me to push the envelope and challenging me to challenge my readers even more. You are a great yin to my yang when it comes to writing.

Finally, thanks to the entire Dare 2 Share team. Your hard work and dedication is resulting in an army of teenagers being equipped to know, live, share, and own their faith. *You rock!*

READ THIS FIRST

This book is not designed to sit on your shelf or to exist under a pile of clothes in your room. It is designed to be a field guide to sharing your faith. Put it in your backpack and take it with you to school. Open it during a lunch and read up a bit and then, when that Wiccan kid or Mormon friend sits down, flip to the back and read up for a minute or two on how you can share Jesus with him in a relevant and nonthreatening way.

In the back of this book (part 3) you'll find out how to share your faith with those who hold the following belief systems:

- Agnosticism
- Atheism
- Buddhism
- Evolution
- Hinduism
- The Watchtower and Tract Society (Jehovah's Witnesses)
- Judaism
- Mormonism
- Islam (Muslim beliefs)
- Wicca (a form of witchcraft)
- And more

But what you are *not* going to find in the back of this book are some kind of spiritual bullets that you can lock and load into your gospel "gun" to blow them away with! Instead, you'll find conversation starters, complements and common ground, the areas you probably agree on and disagree about, a few key passages to focus on in your talk, and some helpful hints.

Part 3 includes more in-depth information about what each of these belief systems hold to and how they often differ from the essentials of Christianity. The last section of this book will be extremely helpful in getting you started creating conversations with those from differing belief systems, and it will help you go even deeper when you find you need more resources. Once a healthy dialogue is going, you can bust out some of the powerful facts of the Christian faith that help other teens reconsider what they believe.

This book will also help you realize that one of the most powerful persuaders when it comes to sharing Jesus is a Spirit-empowered, loving Christian who listens just as much as he or she talks!

But this field guide doesn't stop there. As you read this book you'll also discover the following:

- How to identify your style of sharing Jesus
- How to defend your faith without offending your friend
- How to share the gospel message in a clear and compassionate way
- How to make the message clear and simple
- How to share your own personal story of coming to believe in Jesus
- And much, much more!

When you are done reading this book and learning the principles it explains, you will know how to share your faith anytime, anywhere, with anyone!

Along the way there are some short and helpful parts of this book that will give you insights, information, and encouragement when it comes to sharing Jesus with your friends:

WARNING!
This section will give you a heads-up that will keep you from making a mistake when it comes to sharing Jesus with your friends.

True Confessions
Here's where I share a true story from my own experiences where I messed up sharing the gospel with somebody else.

Can I Get a Witness?
These are true stories or insights from teenagers who are daring to share their faith anytime, anywhere, and with anyone.

The 411
This will give you some tactical and practical help when it comes to Web sites, resources, and ideas to help you become better at sharing your faith with your friends.

So before you get started, realize that when you share Jesus with your friends you are taking them on the journey of a lifetime. This book can become your field guide during this dangerous and exciting adventure. Of course the ultimate field guide is the Word of God itself!

My challenge to you is to read *Dare 2 Share* all the way through once. Take a few hours, sit down, and read the whole thing (believe me, it's easy reading!). Then put it in your backpack to keep with you as a handy reference guide. This will give you easy access to the basic information you need to share your faith with anyone, anytime, anywhere!

But more than anything else, before you get started, pray. Pray that God will move in your heart, soul, and mind to give you the passionate motivation and the practical tools to reach your friends, family, classmates, teammates, and coworkers for Jesus. This life-changing adventure will not only transform your friends, it will change you on the deepest level as well.

Let the journey begin right now!

GETTING

READY

FOR

THE

JOURNEY

PART ONE

CHAPTER 1

DOUG

Doug came from a shattered family in the inner city of Denver where he was raised by his mom. He was reared in a family and a neighborhood where violence, crime, and dysfunction were the norm.

To add to Doug's long list of personal problems, he had a dangerous form of epilepsy. Grand mal seizures were part of the reality he had to live with. On two separate occasions he had such severe seizures that his heart stopped and he nearly died.

Doug also struggled when it came to school. He had a difficult time learning and was a bit slow even when it came to the most basic subjects. Although he tried hard, his best wasn't good enough.

Kids from Doug's school often made fun of him. His epilepsy and learning disabilities made him an easy target. More often than not, Doug responded with his fists. As a result, suspensions from school and trouble with the law followed. Doug was spiraling quickly down a dangerous road of self-destruction.

One day Doug was invited to go to a Christian camp in Florida. He went and the experience changed his life forever. While at this camp he heard speaker after speaker who challenged him to make a difference with his life. They all seemed to be talking straight to him. They confronted him about serving Jesus with his whole heart. They talked about the need to tell others the good news of Jesus so they could be saved from hopelessness now and hell later.

Doug was listening. Although he had put his faith in Christ as a child, that week Doug dedicated his life to follow Jesus Christ with all of his heart and to share the gospel with everybody he met. His resolution was to keep as many people as possible out of hell.

At 16 years old Doug even didn't own a bike, let alone a car. Doug would walk everywhere to speak to as many people as possible about Jesus. It was not uncommon to see Doug sharing with some person waiting at the bus stop or hitchhiking.

Although Doug wasn't super articulate, he continued to share Jesus with everybody he met. Sometimes he would stumble and stammer his way through the gospel message, but people listened. Doug had a sincerity and way about him that won people over. Although he was just a high school kid, he was determined, kind, painfully honest, and genuinely concerned about the people he talked to.

Doug saved up his money and bought a pretty nice bicycle. He was completely excited by his new mobile means of sharing Jesus with others. He rode his bike everywhere, talking to all sorts of people—in parks, on the street, on sidewalks, and across overpasses.

One day he told me the story of pulling up to a stoplight and noticing a car full of guys next to him, waiting for the red light to turn green. He thought, *These guys are going to die and go to hell unless I tell them about Jesus.* So he knocked on the passenger-side window. One of the men tentatively rolled the window down, curious about what this teenager wanted. Doug knew that his time was short, so he shared the gospel message as quickly and clearly as he could. But he couldn't get it out fast enough. The light turned green.

"We gotta go!" the driver blurted as he mashed down the gas pedal to drive away. But Doug wouldn't let the opportunity pass by without a fight. Too much was at stake.

"I am going with you!" he yelled as he grabbed on to the car door handle with his left hand and steered his bike with his right while the car accelerated.

These guys were in shock as Doug continued to share the gospel message. At 20 miles per hour Doug was still talking, almost yelling to be heard above the whizzing sound of passing traffic. At 30 miles per hour he was almost finished sharing the gospel. Finally, at 40 miles per hour Doug was done. With one last challenge he screamed, "I hope you all trust in Jesus and receive the gift of eternal life!"

He released his white-knuckled fingers, and his 10-speed whizzed then slowed then wobbled toward the curb.

When Doug told me what had happened I flatly said, "Doug, you're an idiot! You could have died! You could have gotten caught under the car and been run over!"

I will never forget his response to my rebuke. He simply stated, "It would have been worth it. I don't mind dying as long as those guys hear and believe the gospel message. I just don't want to see those guys go to hell."

Doug was one of those teenagers who took his Christianity seriously. He really believed in heaven and hell. It wasn't a sophisticated faith. It was a simple, childlike trust in God.

But Doug really believed it, and to be honest I felt convicted every time I was around him.

Finally, at age 19 Doug graduated from high school and went off to the "real world," but he never graduated from sharing his faith.

Today Doug is a custodian at a high school in Ankeny, Iowa. Every week or so, he calls me. We talk about all sorts of things, like family, friends, life—that sort of stuff. But inevitably we talk about the people that he is currently trying to lead to Christ.

As a custodian in a high school, Doug gets to share his faith in Jesus all the time . . . and does!

One day at the Judgment Seat of Christ, Doug's name will be called. On that day I believe thousands will stand and applaud this epileptic, socially challenged, struggling custodian for the impact he made on their lives.

I will be one of them. You see, Doug is my big brother. Growing up together, I watched with awe as he overcame all of his inabilities and disabilities to share Jesus with everyone he could. He refused to be excused. I knew if Doug could overcome his fears and insecurities, then so could I.

And so can you.

That's what this book is all about, to help you refuse to be excused, to give you all the tools, motivation, and resources you need to share Jesus with others.

But it all starts with passion. Without a passion to share your faith you won't bother to learn how; you'll probably quit after the first failed attempt.

It's passion for Jesus and for those who don't know Jesus that gave my brother all the fuel he needed to share. So how do you get this kind of passion?

Read on!

CHAPTER 2

PASSION FUEL

I remember the first time that I shared my faith. It was with five or six teenagers at Sloan's Lake in Denver. They were just standing around, so I walked up to them and started asking them questions. Pretty soon we were in a conversation about spiritual things and soon after I was explaining the gospel to them the best that I knew how.

Oh, by the way, I was 10 years old at the time.

That may sound kind of weird, a fifth grader sharing Jesus with a bunch of high school kids out of the blue. But I couldn't help myself. Somebody had given me passion fuel.

What is passion fuel? It is the internal drive and motivation to tell others about Jesus! It is what my brother Doug was driven by. It is what got my engine revved up too!

How do you get passion fuel in your spiritual system? You ask God for it. You search God's Word for it. You seek it with all your heart.

When you stop to think about it, you see passion fuel everywhere. If you have a friend who is really good at sports and excels on the court or the field, he or she is probably tanked up on passion fuel. That is the burning, brewing motivation that sizzles and simmers behind his athletic accomplishments.

For some that passion fuel is comprised of a longing to hear "Way to go!" or "I'm proud of you!" from their dad. For some it is jealousy that fuels their actions. For others it is the desire for a scholarship or popularity at their school.

There are all sorts of motivations that can comprise passion fuel, good ones or bad ones. The point is that everyone who excels at anything is usually propelled by passion fuel of some brand.

My brother and I were energized by passion fuel too. This fuel gave us all the energy we needed to share our faith in spite of our "handicaps," my brother's being his lack of social development and "slowness," mine my age.

Passion fuel can overcome any inability, disability, or excuse. Passion fuel can give you the internal thrust to bust through the perceived barriers that are keeping you from sharing your faith in Jesus.

What are those roadblocks for you?

Maybe you don't know how to share your faith. Don't worry, passion fuel will motivate you to discover how (and reading and applying this book will help too!).

Maybe you are afraid of what your friends will think if you start sharing Jesus with them. Passion fuel will give you the internal motivation to run that fear right over and to share Jesus in spite of the quaver in your voice and knocking in your knees.

Perhaps you are not living a life that backs up your message. You are kind of afraid that if you start sharing Jesus with your friends that they will point out this inconsistency. Passion fuel will give you the strength to start living differently so that what comes out of your life and your lips are not contradicting each other.

Whatever your roadblock, passion fuel will help you drive right through it!

What was the passion fuel that propelled my brother and me? To be honest, there were different kinds at different times. Just as there are different types of gasoline when you pull up to the pump, from regular unleaded to super unleaded, there are several different kinds of passion fuel you can use when it comes to sharing your faith. Among these motivations are obedience to God, compassion for the lost, and the fear of our friends going to hell.

These aren't the only kinds of passion fuel, but they are right at the top of the list. Among other motivations that can propel you is the fear of giving an account to Jesus someday (2 Corinthians 5:10), the rush from getting rewarded by Him for our faithfulness (1 Corinthians 3:11-15), the transformational power the gospel can exert in the lives of unbelievers (Romans 1:16), and so on! There are all sorts of motivations that can become your passion fuel for sharing Jesus with everyone you encounter.

But we are going to focus on three types of fuel that I believe can get you turning and burning down the road toward the finish line faster than anything! I'm going to give you three types of fuel to choose from: Leaded, Unleaded, and Diesel.

1. LEADED PASSION FUEL: BECAUSE GOD WANTS YOU TO

Right before Jesus ascended into heaven He told His disciples, "All authority in heaven and on earth has been given to me. Therefore go and make disciples of all nations, baptizing them in the name of the Father and of the Son and of the Holy Spirit, and teaching them to obey everything I have commanded you. And surely I am with you always, to the very end of the age" (Matthew 28:18-20). Basically, Jesus is telling His disciples (and if you are a follower of Jesus then you are a disciple, too) that we have the right, responsibility, and reason to share the message of Jesus.

We have the right to share this message because Jesus has the authority and has authorized us to go and make disciples out of everybody on this planet! Even in parts of the world where sharing the gospel is illegal we have the right to share our faith. Why? Because the Son of God Himself gave you the right! He earned the right by shedding His blood for our sins!

We have the responsibility to share this message because Jesus commanded us to do it! This passage of Scripture has been nicknamed "the Great Commission," not "the Good Suggestion," for a reason. It is not optional. God Himself is telling you to go and share this message with everybody you can.

We have the reason to share this message because Jesus goes with us! He tells us that He is with us always, even to the end of the age. Stop and think about that for a moment. The God of the universe is with you every second of every day. Jesus is with you at school, when you drive down the street, when you are over at your friend's house, when you are surfing the Internet, and when your are playing sports. He is with you every day and all the time.

If you could see Him would you be embarrassed to introduce Him to your friends? No way! You'd go up to your friends and say, "Hey, I want to introduce you to my best friend, Jesus. Have you two ever met?" If you could see Jesus you would never be embarrassed

> **WARNING!**
>
> Although we have the right to share our faith, we need to make sure that we do it with love and humility. Otherwise, nobody is going to want to hear about it!

to introduce Him to your friends. Okay, brace yourself; this is where it gets a little convicting.

The Bible tells us in 2 Corinthians 5:7 that we should "live by faith, not by sight." In other words, we should live as though we can see the invisible. We should walk by what we know to be true and not just by what we can see with the human eye. How does all this apply to you and sharing the gospel with your friends? Simple: If Jesus tells us that He is with us to the end of the age, then He is with us. We should live like He is right at our side all the time and talk about Him with boldness.

My Cousin Eric

I don't come from a typical religious, Bible-reading, church-going family. I come from a family of bodybuilding, tobacco-chewing, beer-drinking thugs. Many of my cousins and uncles are title-winning bodybuilders. I don't know what happened to me. I got ripped off by the gene pool.

One of my cousins, Eric, is especially big. At one point he could bench press well above 500-pounds. He is 5' 8" tall and about 5' 8" wide. Suffice it to say, he is huge.

One night when I was in high school I was at a popular mall, busy sharing my faith with other teenagers. Two teenage boys I was talking to were especially negative to the message. As I started sharing with them about Jesus they began making fun of me. That was a mistake, a big one.

Eric, who is a believer, was leaning against a wall about 10 feet away, listening in to our conversation. When these two guys started making fun of his scrawny little cousin (that would be me), he slowly lumbered his gigantic frame over to the snickering teens. With pecs flexed and biceps bulging he glared into their eyes and said, "This is my cousin. If you don't listen to what he has got to say you are going to want to know where you will go when you die . . . because you will die."

Suddenly these two poor teenagers were downright "interested" in the gospel message. They smiled and nodded and said they would trust in Christ right away. Trembling and terrified they prayed with me right there in the mall. I don't know if they really became Christians or were just going through the motions because my cousin was standing by my side. All I do know is that I sure liked having Eric right there next to me while I was talking about Jesus. I thought to myself, *If I could just take my cousin Eric with me wherever I went sharing, I would never be afraid again. If someone wouldn't trust in Christ I could just say, "Eric, beat the sin out of them."* Just kidding. I would never do that. But the whole incident made me think about a person and a presence bigger than Eric.

I suddenly realized that the maker of heaven and earth (and Eric) dwells inside of me and goes with me everywhere I go . . . Jesus Christ Himself. When I'm afraid to share my faith I try to reflect on that promise of Jesus' presence, and I am suddenly infused with a new sense of confidence. "I am with you always" . . . always.

He is always there to encourage, coach, strengthen, and enable us. He is always with us. This mind-blowing truth should be a big reason we are sharing our faith. He is with us and He told us in the Great Commission to tell everyone about Him.

2. UNLEADED PASSION FUEL: YOUR FRIENDS NEED JESUS NOW!

Whether they know it or not, your friends need Jesus right now. We as humans were made with an invisible, unquenchable need for God. Life without God is like having a car without an engine, a cell phone without a service provider, or a book without words. It's the existence of God that gives us the basis for hope. It's the love of God that gives us the reason to hope.

If there is a God and that God loved us enough to send His Son to die for our sins, then life is worth living. Why? Because if this God exists then everything we do on this earth matters for eternity!

Can you imagine living a life without the hope of Jesus? Sure, there are some temporary fun fixes—drugs, sexual promiscuity, drinking, and partying, just to name a few. And, yes, there are some "non-sin" pastimes that one can enjoy apart from Jesus—friends, sports, hobbies, clothes, family, to name a few.

But at the core of every non-Christian there is a gaping hole. This hole can be temporarily filled with friends, sports, or sin. But it doesn't stick. Some who recognize this keep trying harder and harder to fill that hole. They try to pack it with more and more escape activities. But no matter how much stuff they stuff into it, it is never fully filled. Why? Because the hole is too big for anything on this side of eternity! The only thing that can truly, fully, and permanently fill that gaping hole is a relationship with Jesus Christ.

From the outside looking in, your friends who don't know Jesus may look happy and fulfilled. They may seem like they have true joy and purpose on this earth. But if you could see into the secret chambers of their soul you would see this black hole of secret longing that can only be filled and fulfilled by Jesus.

When Jesus walked the earth He could see this cold, dark rift in the souls of people. Here's what the Bible says about Jesus' ability to see into the souls of those around Him: "When he saw the crowds, he had compassion on them, because they were harassed and helpless, like sheep without a shepherd" (Matthew 9:36). *Thousands* of people were following Jesus and He could see that black hole of hopelessness in their souls. He felt sorry for them. He hurt for them.

Do you hurt for your friends who don't know Jesus? And what about the crowds of students at your school? Look at them through the eyes of Jesus. Imagine that gaping hole in their souls and then be willing to do whatever it takes to fill it with Jesus.

3. DIESEL PASSION FUEL: THERE'S HELL TO PAY!

I have a confession to make that may surprise you. I have a serious problem with the doctrine of hell. It's hard to imagine a loving God who would create an *eternal* place of suffering for sinners. Don't get me wrong; I think that sinners should suffer some. But an eternity of agony in "fire and brimstone" for all those who happen not to be Christians? Come on!

It's a lot easier to imagine hell as a place where people are not physically tortured but psychologically tormented until they regret and repent. Maybe at this point they are even given a second chance to respond to Christ. This kind of hell seems to have the best of both worlds: Sinners are punished and then mercy is demonstrated. Perhaps the exception to this rule is the worst of the worst sinners. Those who commit mass murder in the name of some warped ideology like Hitler and Stalin can burn forever as far as I'm concerned.

Or maybe hell could be mere annihilation—eternal extinction of the soul, if you will. When people are plunged into that infernal inferno, it is a final purging of existence. Their slates are wiped clean and they cease to be. As horrible as that may sound, it is infinitely more fathomable than an *eternal* hell.

I have a problem with accepting a doctrine that condemns the sinner to a forever future without hope, without escape, without a second chance. To be honest my heart begins to hurt and my brain starts to ache when I think about it. Questions flood my mind and challenge my convictions. Questions like how could a loving God send people to an eternity in fire and brimstone? And if God is so merciful why would He cause people to suffer for so long in such pain?

But no matter how many times I try to explain hell away or redefine it and make it palatable to my puny brain, there it is in black and white again and again throughout the pages of the Bible. No matter how I try to imagine it away or tone it down, one thing is clear: The Bible describes hell as for real and forever.

Jesus throws kerosene on the flames when He speaks so matter-of-factly about a literal hell. Did you know that the Son of God spoke more about hell than heaven? Of the 19 times that hell is mentioned in the New Testament, 12 are mentioned by Jesus. And He never described hell as figurative, temporary, or anything less than horrific. Five different times He calls it a place of "weeping and gnashing of teeth." I'm not even sure what gnashing of teeth means, but it doesn't sound pleasant.

Speaking of unpleasant thoughts, check out these verses about hell:

> "And they will go out and look upon the dead bodies of those who rebelled against me; their worm will not die, nor will their fire be quenched, and they will be loathsome to all mankind." (Isaiah 66:24)

◆

"But the subjects of the kingdom will be thrown outside, into the darkness, where there will be weeping and gnashing of teeth." (Matthew 8:12)

◆

He will punish those who do not know God and do not obey the gospel of our Lord Jesus. They will be punished with everlasting destruction and shut out from the presence of the Lord and from the majesty of his power. (2 Thessalonians 1:8-9)

◆

"[Anyone who worships evil] will drink of the wine of God's fury, which has been poured full strength into the cup of his wrath. He will be tormented with burning sulfur in the presence of the holy angels and of the Lamb. And the smoke of their torment rises for ever and ever. There is no rest day or night." (Revelation 14:10-11)

The list of verses goes on and on and on. From the Old Testament to the New Testament, from the prophets to the apostles to Jesus Himself, hell is described with real and raw adjectives as your worst fears coming true and then multiplied by infinity for eternity.

Here is where the troubling question rears its ugly head once again. How could a loving God send people whom He created to suffer in an eternal hell?

And maybe that question is the problem. Oftentimes the twenty-first-century version of the Christian God is just loving instead of *just* and *loving*. The just part of God (which demands absolute justice, holiness, and perfection) has been minimized and the loving part of God (which shows mercy, grace, and forgiveness) has been maximized. As a result, we have tailored our view into a God who is big on love and light on bite. He becomes more of a cosmic Santa Claus who caters to our every whim, rather than the King of Kings and Lord of Lords.

While most of us Christians believe in some kind of hell, we usually just don't bring it up much. It is an unpleasant subject and leads to too many questions about the character of God. Hell is that crazy doctrine that we keep locked in the basement of our belief systems. We all know that it is there, chained to the underbelly of the theology of the holiness of God. We hope that it stays in the shadows and never comes up in conversation. Why? Because if people found out what we really believed they would think we were radicals, extremists, and kooks. If hell isn't real, then maybe we are.

But if it is real, then why aren't we more intense, more aggressive, more intentional, more urgent? If hell is real (and the Bible

CAN I GET A WITNESS?

My name is Chelsi! I am 16 years old and I live in Fairborn, Ohio! I attended a Dare 2 Share conference and wasn't expecting my life to change as much as it did in a matter of two days! I watched the drama "Letter from Hell" and I took the 48-hour challenge [to share my faith with someone within 48 hours]. Honestly I thought it would be the hardest thing to do, but when I walked into school on Monday I looked at people as if they were burning in hell! I could not stand it. I could not believe I was letting my friends go to hell! From that weekend on, I opened a conversation up about God and His Son Jesus Christ every chance I could get! Many people have given their hearts to the Lord this year, and it wouldn't have happened if I hadn't told them the GOSPEL!

says it is) then we should be motivated to keep as many people as we can out of it—friends, foes, teachers, classmates, coworkers, teammates, family members, strangers . . . everybody.

I SAW THE SIGN

When I was 12 years old my youth leader, Tim Sanchez, gave me a morbid homework assignment. He told me to go to a local mall on a Saturday afternoon and just sit on a bench at a busy section and watch people for 30 minutes. As I watched them I was supposed to imagine a small sign on their foreheads with the words "Bound for Hell" written across it. This whole thing sounded kind of weird to me, but I did it anyway.

I walked to the Westminster Mall, which was only a mile or so away from my house. Once in, I made my way around the mall for a few minutes trying to find the best place to sit down and begin my "homework." Once I found the right spot I sat down, settled in, and started looking at people intently, trying to imagine those eerie words scrawled across the foreheads of those who passed by. At first I felt stupid and self-conscious. People were watching me watch them and it felt uncomfortable. But in a few minutes I was well into my imagination exercise.

In those 30 minutes my life changed forever.

I watched young and old, geeks and freaks, herds of nerds and flocks of jocks, blue-haired elderly women and blue-haired pierced skaters, swaggering mall security guards and staggering old men, moms trying to catch their toddlers on the run and dads trying to catch a nap on the benches. Not only did I imagine these people bound for a literal hell, I imagined their lives, apart from Christ, as a living hell. This was the closest I ever came to understanding

Matthew 9:36, "When he saw the crowds, he had compassion on them, because they were harassed and helpless, like sheep without a shepherd." Jesus had His own imagination exercise. He envisioned the throngs of people that were following Him as sheep without a shepherd . . . scared, confused, and in danger.

The word "compassion" means to suffer with, to enter into somebody else's pain. That's what happened to Jesus on the hillside 2,000 years ago and to me at the mall 27 years ago. It's almost as though God peeled back the curtain and allowed me to feel their hurts and see their pain. I imagined their lives and afterlives without Christ and it broke my heart.

I never viewed people the same after that. I still see the sign. When I'm at the airport waiting in the security line I see the sign. When I'm sitting in traffic and turn to see the guy in the car next to me I see the sign. When I'm standing in front of thousands of screaming teenagers at a Dare 2 Share conference I see the sign. When I'm sitting at a Starbucks (like I am now) and see the man next to me sipping his latte and looking out the window (like he is now) I see the sign. I can't get it out of my brain.

The sign keeps me up at night, wakes me up in the middle of the night and gets me out of bed in the morning. It drives me to do what it takes to raise up an army of teenagers, youth leaders, parents, and pastors who see the sign too.

I saw the sign, and it opened up my eyes.

What now? Why not go to a busy mall on a crowded Saturday afternoon all by yourself and watch people for 30 minutes. Find a seat and see the "Bound for Hell" signs plastered on passing foreheads. Imagine how miserable their lives might be and their afterlives will be without Jesus. Feel their pain. Don't leave until you do. When you are finished, write a letter to God recording your thoughts and feelings. Keep that letter as a reminder of this powerful and dramatic exercise of the imagination.

Fifteen years ago, after thinking about hell and the average teenager's unwillingness to keep their friends out of it, I wrote the following poem, "Don't Bother Me." As you read it, perhaps you will catch glimpses of your own apathy and excuses. But more

CONFESSIONS

TRUE

Okay, okay, so I saw the sign. But there were times that in the midst of my busy schedule I forgot about it. It took Liz to remind me. She was the shift manager of the restaurant where I used to prepare sermons when I was a pastor. I saw her almost every morning. We talked politely. She knew I was a pastor and I knew that she knew. I kept thinking that I would bring the gospel up later. Later never came. One day I came into the restaurant and Liz wasn't there to greet me. So I seated myself in my normal booth and began to study. Sarah, the waitress who worked the same shift as Liz, began pouring coffee in my cup as my head was buried in my Bible. I noticed her hand was trembling as she poured the coffee. Looking up I noticed a tear streaming down her cheek. I asked what was wrong. "Oh, haven't you heard?" she sobbed. "Last night Liz killed herself."

I was stunned. Liz seemed like an intelligent, mentally stable middle-aged lady. But underneath her smiling façade a cauldron of worthless feelings had been stirred by the finger of the Devil. A tear came streaming down my cheek at that moment. Not just because I lost a friend, but because I missed an opportunity, countless opportunities, to tell her about Jesus.

I was too busy preparing sermons to see the sign.

Never again.

important, I hope you will step up to its challenge and acknowl-
edge the gut-wrenching reality that how you answer the question
"Why bother?" has consequences for all eternity.

Don't Bother Me
Don't bother me with souls to save.
I have my own agenda.
There's school to do, sports to play,
Important stuff to attend to.

Don't bother me with that little girl,
The girl playing by the street.
She's much too young to understand
The Savior she could meet.

Don't bother me with my friend at school.
He's got his own religion.
I don't have time to change his mind.
He'll make his own decision.

Don't bother me with distant sounds I hear,
The sounds of people screaming.
Although I wonder who they are.
What are these victims shrieking?

Don't bother me with who they are.
I really don't want the blame.
For it's the little girl and my friend at school
Who from hell scream out my name . . .
    But don't bother me.

Why bother sharing the gospel with everyone you can? God told you to, your friends need Jesus now, and there's hell to pay if they don't hear the gospel and believe it.

What Revs Your Engine?

Which kind of passion fuel revs your engine and gets your motivational motor running? Maybe you are more driven out of your love for Jesus and you want to share Christ because He told you to! If it's compassion for your friends now or fear of hell for them later, then fill 'er up! If it's something else, then top it off with that passion fuel. Leaded, Unleaded, Diesel, or otherwise, you need a motivational fuel so that you can put the pedal to the metal and let her rip!

CHAPTER 3

GET STRONG

You can't share Jesus without Jesus! You'll chicken out, freak out, or burn out without His power, protection, and guidance. Maybe that's why these are the last words of Jesus before He ascended into the skies: "But **you will receive power when the Holy Spirit comes on you**; and you will be my witnesses in Jerusalem, and in all Judea and Samaria, and to the ends of the earth" (Acts 1:8).

Jesus is telling His disciples that when they received the Holy Spirit they would also receive power, explosive power, to share the good news about Jesus everywhere they went. The same is true of us. So the question is this: Have you received the Holy Spirit? If you are not sure, check this verse out: "And you also were included in Christ when you heard the word of truth, the gospel of your salvation. **Having believed, you were marked in him with a seal, the promised Holy Spirit**" (Ephesians 1:13).

According to this verse, if you have put your faith and trust in Jesus Christ (based on His dying for your sins) then you have received the Holy Spirit. And if you have received the Holy Spirit then you have all of His power at your disposal to give you the courage, strength, and wisdom you need to tell your friends about Jesus.

JUMPER-CABLE CHRISTIANS VERSUS SPIRIT-CHARGED SUPER SAINTS

Have you ever tried to start a car with a dead battery? No fun. That's where jumper cables come in handy. You take one side and connect it to a fully charged battery and the other side and connect it to the dead battery. After a few minutes the dead battery should be charged and ready to start again.

The problem is that many Christian teenagers view the power of God in them like a battery that needs constant recharging. These jumper-cable Christians go to youth group and get a jolt. After a day or two the charge dies down so they need to go back to church for another volt and jolt. Camps are like a full charge that lasts for a week or two. The charge from a mission trip sometimes lasts for a month.

Many Christian teenagers look for spiritual high after spiritual high to carry them through their earthly lives. They go to church or youth group and mentally fasten one end of their spiritual jumper cables to their pastor's pulpit or youth leader's music stand and they fasten the other end to what they think is a dead spiritual battery in their hearts. They hope that the charge will carry them through the week. But it won't. Why? Because emotional jolts of temporary inspiration aren't enough to give you the boldness and wisdom you need to reach your friends. You need a sustained current of spiritual strength. You need to become a Spirit-Charged Super Saint.

What does that mean? Imagine an electrical outlet right in

the middle of your chest. That outlet is the Spirit of God. If you choose to plug into Him through prayer, He will give you a sustained current of spiritual power to share the gospel with anybody you encounter and live a life that supports the message you are sharing. But you have to plug into His power through faith.

The apostle Paul wrote these words to the Christians who lived in Ephesus: "I pray that out of his glorious riches he may strengthen you with **power through his Spirit in your inner being**" (Ephesians 3:16). Notice that this is not just strength. It is mighty inner strength that God provides through His Holy Spirit.

We don't need a moving sermon or song to get it. We don't need to be standing around a campfire after a week of hearing sermons at some Christian camp. We don't need to even feel like it. All we need to get this power is to plug in through prayer and faith. As soon as you ask for God's strength He gives it to you. Although you may not feel some spiritual sensation reverberating,

CAN I GET A WITNESS?

My name is Madelyn. I'm 13 and from St. Louis, Missouri. After I went to a Dare 2 Share conference last year I really wanted to witness to my dad but did not have the strength to do it on my own. I realized that I need the Holy Spirit to guide me and to give me the courage to lead him to Christ. All through the Bible there are stories of how the Holy Spirit can do amazing things if we just let Him. Witnessing to my dad was a mountain in my journey, but with the Holy Spirit inside of me it's only a bump in the road.

the Spirit is there nonetheless. He will give you the strength you need to live and share your faith in power as a Spirit-Charged Super Saint.

And you are going to need that power because you are going to face a dark force that will do everything it can to keep you from sharing Jesus.

CHAPTER 4

BEWARE THE DARKNESS

If you choose to share your faith and especially if you do it drenched in the Holy Spirit's power, beware. A dark force will be unleashed against your efforts that will do everything in its wicked, scheming power to stop you. The kingdom of darkness will muster its evil powers on a quest to defeat your efforts and discourage you enough so that you will surrender.

Satan and his army of fallen angels will do everything in their underestimated power to get you to quit. They will attempt to destroy. If they can't, they will, at the very least, try to deceive, distract, and discourage you.

How? They'll whisper in your ear things like, "Hey, don't go pushing your religion on your friends. Build the relationship a little bit longer before you bring it up. And by the way, you have some areas in your life that need to be corrected before you go out and share Jesus. Just wait. It will all work out in God's perfect timing."

If that doesn't work they'll distract you with sports, work, hobbies, relationships, studies—anything and everything. They'll do their best to keep you so busy that you forget people need Jesus—that without Him they are "harassed and helpless, like sheep without a shepherd" (Matthew 9:36).

These demonic entities may lie to you with thoughts like, *"Are you even sure about this whole thing called Christianity yourself? I mean, come on, you are putting your faith in a man you've never met, who lived, died, and supposedly rose from the dead two thousand years ago. You are staking your eternal destiny on some dude named Jesus who claimed to be some kind of God-man. You better be sure yourself before you try pushing this wacky belief on somebody else."*

Maybe what they'll do is discourage you. They'll remind you of your cruddy home life or the fact that you don't have a boyfriend or girlfriend. Perhaps they will whisper lies in your ears when you step on the scale or look in the mirror. They'll try to tell you you're too fat, too ugly, too skinny, too zitty, too whatever.

Don't buy the lies.

Demons are just doing what they do. Their purpose is to sidetrack the divine plan of advancing the kingdom of God through His children. If our purpose is to glorify God, their purpose is to "de-glorify" Him. The last thing Satan and his army of naughty

CONFESSIONS

TRUE

I went through a time in my life where I rebelled against the Great Commission. I bought the lies of Satan that if I just lived a godly life in front of other teenagers they would see it, ask me about it, and trust in Christ. After months of trying this I realized that nobody was noticing, nobody was asking, nobody was coming to Christ. So I started bringing Jesus up again while still seeking to live a life that backed up my message. What I realized is that it is not either/or, either sharing Jesus with my life or with my lips. It took both/and, both living the message and sharing it.

angels wants is for your friends, classmates, teammates, and neighbors to come to Christ.

WHO IS SATAN?

Satan is a real being. He was created by God to be an angel—as a matter of fact, the top angel of God. Here's how God describes him, as told by the prophet Ezekiel:

> "You were the model of perfection,
> full of wisdom and perfect in beauty.
> You were in Eden,
> the garden of God;
> every precious stone adorned you:
> ruby, topaz and emerald,
> chrysolite, onyx and jasper,
> sapphire, turquoise and beryl.
> Your settings and mountings were made of gold;
> on the day you were created they were prepared.
> You were anointed as a guardian cherub,
> for so I ordained you.
> You were on the holy mount of God;
> you walked among the fiery stones.
> You were blameless in your ways
> from the day you were created
> till wickedness was found in you." (Ezekiel 28:12-15)

The Devil was created to be God's personal bodyguard (why He would need one, I don't know!). He was perfect in wisdom, beautiful to look at, and indescribably powerful. He had it all—

huge pecs, a high IQ, and a dazzling smile. And maybe that was the problem. At some point maybe he caught a glimpse of himself in a golden heavenly mirror. Moments later he was posing and flexing and thinking, "You are one handsome, strong, and smart dude. If you applied yourself, you could climb the corporate ladder here in heaven. As a matter of fact, I bet the angels in heaven would follow you and you could completely take over this place. All you have to do is dethrone the Son of God."

CAN I GET A WITNESS?

My name is Andrea! I am 17 years old and from Stewartville, Minnesota. I really wanted to try talking to my friends [about Jesus]. I began praying and about a week later a friend from work just sat down and began telling me that he was really down and a lot of bad stuff was going on in his life. He continued to tell me how he was going to go home that night and get drunk so that he could forget about all of his problems. I thought—*perfect opportunity to talk to him about God.* But then the Enemy came in and started telling me he won't listen, he's not going to care, he's probably going to go off and tell all the other guys at work what I said and make fun of me. But I remembered that all those thoughts were just the Enemy trying to stop me, so I said a little prayer in my head asking God to give me strength to speak up and I did. About a month later he started to go to my youth group and he accepted Jesus Christ. After that he talked his brother into coming too. I learned not to listen to the Enemy and how to recognize when the thoughts are mine and when they're not. We can fight the Enemy with God's help.

Whatever the exact conversation that Satan had with himself was, he convinced himself that he could plan a mutiny among the angels that would end up with his ruling and Jesus looking for a new job. Here's how the book of Isaiah describes what happened:

> You said in your heart,
> "I will ascend to heaven;
> I will raise my throne
> above the stars of God;
> I will sit enthroned on the mount of assembly,
> on the utmost heights of the sacred mountain.
> I will ascend above the tops of the clouds;
> I will make myself like the Most High."
> But you are brought down to the grave,
> to the depths of the pit. (Isaiah 14:13-15)

The Devil gathered a third of the angels to help him take over heaven. He launched his short-lived mutiny. Suffice it to say that

CONFESSIONS

TRUE

One time when I was a teenager I dared the Devil to attack me. I thought that just because I was a child of God there was no way that he could ever defeat me. I was wrong. Even children of God need to be walking in the power of God to win against Satan and sin. After triple-dog daring the Devil, I went through a season of extreme trouble and temptation in my life. Why? I think God let Satan attack me to humble me and make me more dependent on Jesus. Lesson? Don't taunt the Devil. Fight him in the power of God, not your own strength.

instead of ruling in heaven he and all of his fellow rebels got thrown out. Now these invisible enemies roam and comb the earth, seeking to use mankind to carry the mutiny on every day.

Their biggest victories come when they keep God's children (that's you and me) from living and sharing our faith. Believe me, they are working overtime to keep your life and your mouth self-centered and quiet about Jesus.

HOW DO WE DEFEAT THE DEVIL?

James 4:7 tells us how to defeat the Devil every time and anytime he attacks: "Submit yourselves, then, to God. Resist the devil, and he will flee from you."

There is a two-step process you must go through to win against him. First of all, submit to God. Choose to put yourself under God's full command; surrender to Him with all of your heart. It's when you choose to do this that you are filled with the power that comes from the Holy Spirit. Satan can't stand against this divine power. He can stand against your strength, but he can't stand against God's power. Second, resist the Devil. That means you push back, say "no," and refuse to give in to his bully words. When you submit to God and resist the Devil, he will run away from you every time, guaranteed.

Don't worry. He'll be back soon. That's okay. You'll be waiting to shove him in the chest once again in the power of God. Here's some encouragement from Scripture:

> Finally, be strong in the Lord and in his mighty power. Put on the full armor of God so that you can take your stand against the devil's schemes. For our struggle is not

against flesh and blood, but against the rulers, against the authorities, against the powers of this dark world and against the spiritual forces of evil in the heavenly realms. (Ephesians 6:10-12)

One of the areas where Satan may attack you is in your confidence in knowing what and why you believe. Read on to discover if he is using this attack strategy on you.

I wrote a book called *Battle Zone* a few years ago through Moody Publishing. It's all about who Satan is and how teenagers can arm themselves to win against him. Check out the store at www.dare2share.org to purchase one.

CHAPTER 5

KNOWING THAT YOU CAN KNOW AND WHAT YOU DO KNOW

I'll never forget the conversation in McDonald's that day. The other guy was drinking a cup of hot coffee and sitting in a booth. I think I ordered a number-one combo with a Coke. To be honest, I forget how the conversation started but pretty soon we were engaged in a full-on discussion about God. It went something like this:

> Guy: "How do you know there's truth?"
>
> Me: "We all exist on the basis of certain truths. We don't jump off of tall buildings because of the truth about gravity. We do fly in airplanes because of the truth about aerodynamics. There are truths that work in relationships like forgiveness, honesty, and loyalty. There are truths in everything. We exist by truth."
>
> Guy: "How do we know that we are not the figment of somebody else's imagination? How do you even know you're even right here? How do I know I'm really here?"
>
> Me: "Let me pour your hot coffee in your lap and you'll know you're here."

We talked for a while longer. He didn't trust in Christ as his Savior right on the spot, but I hope I made him take a second look at Jesus and the claims of Christ.

The conversation I had with that guy represents the kind of philosophical conflict many Christian teenagers are facing with their non-Christian friends. The comment I most often get from teenagers goes something like, "Well, that's true for you. My truth is a little different."

Really?

Do you have a different truth when it comes to gravity? If so, why not take a flying leap off the Empire State Building? I'll be waiting at the bottom with a scooper and a body bag!

Truth is truth. It's not dependent on your perspective or acceptance of it. Truth is truth with or without you.

Truth is not a popularity contest. If 99 out of 100 people believe that black is white and up is down, up does not become down and black does not become white.

The same is true with spiritual truth. If Jesus is God then Allah is not, Joseph Smith was wrong, and Buddha is in trouble. If Jesus is not God then He was a kook. Why? Because He claimed to be God! He told His disciples in John 10:30, "I and the Father are one." In other words, Jesus Christ is every bit as much God as the heavenly Father is!

Not only that, but Jesus claimed to be the only way to get to heaven. Listen to His words in John 14:6: "I am the way and the truth and the life. No one comes to the Father except through me."

Notice the word that Jesus uses and which one He doesn't. He claims to be *the* way, not *a* way; *the* truth, not *a* truth; *the* life, not *a* life.

The whole "well, that's true for you" argument doesn't fly with Jesus. He is the Author of truth and what He speaks is truth.

TRUTH, PROOF, AND FAITH

If there is truth can we know it for sure? What about proof? Can I really prove my Christianity? Where does faith come in?

All of these are great and relevant questions, especially in a culture where we are encouraged to each have our own customized versions of personal truth. While nobody except God Himself knows all truth, there are some spiritual truths that we can know for sure.

The key word here is "enough." He gives us enough proof so that we can respond in faith and believe Him. In legal language it's called "a preponderance of evidence." Basically, this means that what a jury needs is *enough* evidence to convict or acquit somebody. They don't need more or less, just enough.

God gives us enough evidence in areas we can test Him in (such as fulfilled prophecies and archaeological, historical, and scientific evidences of the Bible's validity) to trust Him in the areas we can't test Him in (heaven, hell, spiritual truth in the invisible realm, etc.). In this preponderance of evidence we have all we need to believe.

If you have a friend who says, "I want proof that God is there!" you can show him the creation, evidence of His existence. You can show him hundreds of fulfilled prophecies from the Old Testament. You can demonstrate the reliability of the Bible in all areas.

But let's say he says, "Well if God is real then why doesn't He come down right now and prove it?" What do you do then? You can tell him two things. The first is that He did do that once when

Jesus became the God-man. The second is that if He "came down" every time an unbeliever wanted proof, then where would faith come in?

God gives us enough evidence so that we can take the next step of faith in full confidence that He is there. But this step is not a leap into the darkness. It's a step into the light!

What does this mean for you?

It simply means that there are certain truths you can know. What Jesus says is truth you can take as truth. And since the Spirit of Jesus inspired the writers of the Bible, then you can take what they wrote in the holy Scriptures as truth as well.

Does that mean that we can know all truth? No way! Our brains are too puny to hold it all. Only God knows all truth.

But we can know some truth. And the sum of the truth that we can know with confidence is what God's Word clearly states. For instance, here are four core truths that the Bible emphasizes again and again.

1. God: You can know that there is a God, the Trinity if you will, one God in three: the Father, Son, and Holy Spirit. While we can't quite comprehend it, we accept it by faith and can know it with certainty. Here are a few verses that will help you know: Deuteronomy 6:4, Isaiah 45:5, Matthew 3:16-17, Ephesians 4:4-6. This God is holy (hates sin) and merciful (loves sinners), and always does what is right and just. He created everything in this universe and is holding it all together by the word of His power (Colossians 1:16-17). He sees everywhere, knows everything, and can do anything. He has always been here and will always be here. His name is "I AM" and because He is, we are!

2. Jesus, God's Son: You can know that Jesus is God. He claimed to be God (John 10:28-30; 14:9), did miracles that could only be done by God (Matthew 8:23-27), and was recognized as God by those around Him (John 1:1, 14, 18). The ultimate proof that Jesus was God was His resurrection from the dead. He was seen by over 500 witnesses over the course of 40 days. If each of these witnesses testified in a court of law for 30 minutes, that would be 250 hours of testimony—that's 10 straight days of testimony. In the average court of law two or three solid witnesses are enough to convict or acquit. Jesus had more than 500 credible witnesses who were willing to risk their lives to say they had just seen Jesus. You can know that Jesus was and is God.

3. The Bible: You can know that the Bible is God's Word, that it is fully trustworthy on every subject it refers to, from geography to archaeology to prophecy . . . anything that ends in a "y" (or any letter for that matter!). The Bible was written by 40 men over a period of 1,500 years. What are the chances of a group of guys, most of whom had never met each other, could write 66 books (that's how many "books" or sections are in the bigger book that we call "the Bible") without contradictions? The chances are zilch, unless God Himself oversaw, guided, and inspired the whole process. According to 2 Peter 1:20-21 and 2 Timothy 3:16-17, He did just that with the book that we call the Bible. This book itself is a miracle of God! It is packed full of fulfilled prophecies that are specific and spectacular!

4. The Gospel: You can know that Jesus died so you can have eternal life. The word *gospel* means "good news." It's the good news that Jesus died for our sins, rose again from the dead, and offers eternal life to all those who trust in Him alone for the forgiveness of their sins! The Bible makes it clear that God wants you to know that you have eternal life. Check this verse out in 1 John 5:13: "I write these things to you who believe in the name of the Son of God so that you may know that you have eternal life."

When you trust in Jesus you can know that you are in a personal, permanent relationship with the God of the universe, no doubt about it!

Why is it important you know that you can know these things? Because according to Hebrews 11:1, "Faith is being sure of what we hope for and certain of what we do not see." In other words, if you can't be certain about some things then you can't have faith! Faith is being sure. It is being certain. It is being confident that what God says in His book is absolutely true!

Although you can't know everything, there are some things

WARNING!

The temptation may be to think, *Isn't all this trusting in Jesus for salvation a little too easy?* But how easy is it to trust in a person you've never met (Jesus) to take you to a place you've never been (heaven)? How easy is it to stake your life and your eternal destiny on a man who lived 2,000 years ago and claimed to be God Himself? It's so easy that a child could do it and it's so hard that a self-righteous adult could choke on it. The reason that receiving the gift of eternal life is so simple and so "easy" is that Jesus did all the work for us. Maybe that's why He reminds us in Titus 3:5, "He saved us, not because of righteous things we had done, but because of his mercy. He saved us through the washing of rebirth and renewal by the Holy Spirit." It's not our hard work, but the hard work of Jesus, that saved us from sin. That's why it is so easy. . . . Jesus did all the work! We simply receive it by faith!

you can be absolutely certain are true. Among these truths are the existence of a personal and powerful God; the reliability of the Bible; that Jesus came, lived, died, and rose again; and that the gospel message is our means of eternal life!

These are truths we can have full confidence in! There are some truths we can be sure of, and there are some that we really don't have a clue about! Let's stand on what we know, share Jesus in humility with others, and continue to lean on God and learn more about Him as we grow in our walk with the Lord.

CAN I GET A WITNESS?

My name is Kelcy. I am 15 years old and from Lincoln, Nebraska. It's by faith alone in Jesus alone that I'm forgiven— wow! For me, the idea that I have forgiveness just because of faith alone is such a hard concept to understand yet completely mind-blowing. Here I am, a sinner, a rugged, unworthy sinner and because I made a decision to have faith that Jesus died for my sins, I get the amazing gift of forgiveness. It doesn't seem like it should be that simple—but the beauty of simplicity is what makes me fall in love with Jesus that much more.

CHAPTER 6

SHARING YOUR FAITH WITH STYLE

What do you think of when you hear the word *style*? If you are like most teenagers you probably think of clothes. Your style is mostly demonstrated by the types of clothes you wear. If you buy your clothes from Abercrombie & Fitch you have one style. If you buy your clothes from Hot Topic you have a very different one.

Everybody's style is different and personal.

The same is true when it comes to sharing your faith. You have a specialized and supernaturally designed style of sharing that you must discover.

Your sharing style is determined through a combination of your personality, spiritual gifting, and emotional maturity. I believe that your style of sharing the gospel can change over the years as you continue to grow personally and spiritually.

DEBBIE AND ME

When I met Debbie I was blown away. She had the three G's that every spiritually oriented Christian guy is looking for: Good, Godly, and Gorgeous! The more I got to know her, the more I was impressed. She loved God and loved others. The question was, would she love me? It took a while, but she finally came around.

After almost four years of dating we finally got married. Like many newlywed couples, we had a lot of conflict in our first few years of marriage. Some of these arguments came over our styles of sharing our faith.

You see, I had a pretty aggressive style of sharing Jesus. I loved to just bring Him up to others, especially teenagers. I found 12- to 18-year-olds especially open to talking about spiritual truths. From the time I was in junior high throughout much of my college career, I used to go to local shopping malls with my Christian friends and create conversations with teenagers about Jesus. More often than not I found teenagers were open to talk, share, debate, and sometimes believe!

Debbie didn't want to have anything to do with my style of evangelism. When she went to the mall she didn't think "sharing with the lost"; she thought "shop till you drop!"

We got into some arguments over the whole thing. She thought I was too pushy with my faith. I thought she was kind of wimpy about hers.

But then God taught me a lesson, a big one.

Debbie has been a fifth-grade public school teacher for years. In one school year, many years ago, she had the opportunity to lead 21 kids to Christ and brought five families out to our church! What is more, she never got one complaint, even from the anti-Christian parents. Why? For one she did it all within the law (and mostly outside the classroom!). Another reason, the bigger reason, is that my wife may be the most loving, kind, and listening person you'll ever meet. Everybody, I mean everybody, loves her. Why? Because she cares about others and listens to them! She listens to them so much that when she talks about Jesus they listen to her!

After watching my wife's effectiveness as a follower of Jesus, I began to realize that there are different ways to share the message of Jesus. I began to do an intense study of the New Testament to discover the various styles of sharing one's faith. I discovered four. There may be more that I missed, but these four styles are the most obvious ways that the early Christians communicated the gospel message with others. Here are the styles that I discovered:

TALKERS, "STALKERS," BUDDIES, AND BRAINS

Let's take a look at each of these four styles and the corresponding New Testament person who best represents that style. Then we'll have you take a test to determine your personal sharing style.

Talkers

Talkers are creative, funny, and easy to talk to. They are usually the life of the party and center of the conversation. They control the conversation, not by force but by sheer wit. When it comes to sharing Jesus with others, they share the gospel in persuasive ways. What's their weakness? Because they are so people-centered and want to be liked, they sometimes can hold back because they are afraid to offend the person they are talking to at the moment.

Who is a biblical example of this style of sharing Jesus? Philip. Let me refresh your memory about this early follower of Jesus through this passage from the Bible that clearly shows his style of sharing Jesus:

> Now an angel of the Lord said to Philip, "Go south to the road—the desert road—that goes down from Jerusalem

to Gaza." So he started out, and on his way he met an Ethiopian eunuch, an important official in charge of all the treasury of Candace, queen of the Ethiopians. This man had gone to Jerusalem to worship, and on his way home was sitting in his chariot reading the book of Isaiah the prophet. The Spirit told Philip, "Go to that chariot and stay near it."

Then Philip ran up to the chariot and heard the man reading Isaiah the prophet. "Do you understand what you are reading?" Philip asked.

"How can I," he said, "unless someone explains it to me?" So he invited Philip to come up and sit with him.

The eunuch was reading this passage of Scripture:

"He was led like a sheep to the slaughter,
and as a lamb before the shearer is silent,
so he did not open his mouth.
In his humiliation he was deprived of justice.
Who can speak of his descendants?
For his life was taken from the earth."

The eunuch asked Philip, "Tell me, please, who is the prophet talking about, himself or someone else?" Then Philip began with that very passage of Scripture and told him the good news about Jesus.

As they traveled along the road, they came to some water and the eunuch said, "Look, here is water. Why shouldn't I be baptized?" And he gave orders to stop the chariot. Then both Philip and the eunuch went down into the water and Philip baptized him. (Acts 8:26-38)

It's easy to see why Philip is such a great example of a Talker. He walked by the carriage and created a natural conversation based on what the Ethiopian eunuch was interested in. He asked nonthreatening questions, started the discussion where the eunuch was at, and then explained the gospel story in a very natural and compelling way. The story was so gripping that when the Ethiopian finally got it, he wanted to pull over right away and get baptized as a Christian!

Talkers know how to "walk along beside the carriage" of their friends, listen for opportunities to bring up the gospel, and bring it up in a persuasive way. If you, like Philip, are a Talker, start looking for those everyday opportunities to bring up the gospel with your friends.

"Stalkers"

Many of the most successful people in the universe were stalkers. And, no, I'm not talking about that evil kind of stalking where someone follows another person. I'm talking about those who stalk a singular goal relentlessly. You have stalker friends who win in sports, studies, and life because they are focused, bold, confident, and determined.

There are Stalkers in the faith-sharing world as well. They tend to be direct, blunt, and strong as they share the gospel. They are thought-provoking by their sheer boldness. What is their primary weakness? Sometimes they can turn people off with their bluntness and boldness.

The apostle Paul was a Stalker of sorts. He was the first one to speak up and the last one to shut up when it came to sharing his faith. Push him down, and he'd get back up. Throw rocks at him, and he'd bandage his wounds and go back in for more. He was unstoppable in sharing Jesus.

While Paul could be extremely creative in presenting Jesus (see Acts 17:16-34), he was usually pretty bold and blunt in his sharing style. The results? Thousands came to Christ and thousands rejected him. Paul had a way of bringing people to a decision, either way, on the spot.

If you are a Stalker, you need to balance your sharing with love (as Paul did more and more, the older he got) but realize that God has called you to be one of those catalytic proclaimers of truth who bring people to a decision through their unrelenting boldness.

Buddies

Buddies are those, like my wife, who are intensely and immensely relational. Sometimes Buddies confuse themselves with Talkers, but they are totally different. While Talkers love to . . . well, talk, Buddies love to listen. In the baseball world they would be more fielders than pitchers. They react to conversations instead of creating them.

When it comes to sharing the gospel, Buddies let the conversation unfold and gently guide it to Jesus. They ask a lot of questions and share a lot fewer answers. They share the message of Christ by tiny degrees in the midst of a conversation (or several) instead of in bold declarations.

While there are several examples of Buddies in the Bible, there is one example, a guy named Barnabas (whose name actually means "son of encouragement"), who was really good at being a buddy. Check this passage out:

> When he [Saul] came to Jerusalem, he tried to join the disciples, but they were all afraid of him, not believing that he really was a disciple. But Barnabas took him and brought him to the apostles. He told them how Saul on

his journey had seen the Lord and that the Lord had spoken to him, and how in Damascus he had preached fearlessly in the name of Jesus. (Acts 9:26-27)

So here's the deal. Before the great apostle Paul was the apostle
Paul, he was a religious leader named Saul. He hated, persecuted,
and chased Christians all over the place. But when Jesus showed
up and knocked him off his donkey, so to speak, Saul became a
Christian. Not only was his soul changed, but so was his name.
Saul became Paul.

So the newly converted Paul came to Jerusalem, the center of
Christianity at that time, and tried to hang out with the other
believers. Nobody wanted to. Most of them knew Paul when he
was Saul, a persecutor of the church. Many of them probably
thought that his conversion to Christianity was some kind of ploy
to get on the inside of the church and really wreak havoc.

Nobody else but Barnabas listened to him. Barnabas took time
to hear Paul's story and
believed him. As a matter of
fact, Barnabas is the one who
took Paul and brought him
personally to appear before
the apostles to share his story
with them.

Almost every time you see
Barnabas in the book of Acts,
he is fighting for the under-
dog. He is the one who listens
to, loves, and empathizes with
those around him.

> # WARNING!
>
> These styles of sharing the
> gospel are not hard and fast.
> You may find yourself as a
> combination of a few of them.
> The goal is to minimize your
> weaknesses, maximize your
> strengths, and use your style
> to advance the good news of
> Jesus while finding balance in
> your own style of evangelism.

While we don't ever see his sharing style per se, we can see clearly that he had a Buddy-bent. You can be sure that he was relational, loved to listen and serve, and shared the gospel in compassionate ways.

My wife is a Buddy. Her strength is that she loves and listens. Her weakness is that sometimes she is afraid to bring up the gospel with others.

If you are a Buddy you are blessed with a huge capacity for loving and listening. People love to talk to you because you love to listen—to *genuinely* listen—to them. You must resist the temptation to just listen. If you are going to become effective for Christ in sharing your faith, you must learn how to gently turn those conversations toward Jesus, as a fielder, not a pitcher; as a Barnabas, not a Paul.

Brains

Brains tend to be smart, organized, and intellectually stimulating (that leaves me out!). They are usually good when it comes to discussing and debating the claims of Christianity.

Luke was a Brain. He wrote two books of the Bible: Luke (duh!) and Acts. What is more, he wrote them to one guy, a Roman official named Theophilus. It seems as though Luke is making a case for Christianity in his first book (Luke) and is demonstrating that it exploded across the world in his second (Acts). Look how Luke describes his own style when it comes to communicating truth:

Many have undertaken to draw up an account of the things that have been fulfilled among us, just as they were handed down to us by those who from the first were eyewitnesses and servants of the word. Therefore, since I myself have carefully investigated everything from the beginning, it seemed good also to me to write an orderly account for you, most excellent Theophilus, so that you may know the certainty of the things you have been taught. (Luke 1:1-4)

Notice the phrases "carefully investigated everything" and "write an orderly account" and "that you may know the certainty of the things." In these phrases you see Luke's style. He studied. He was organized in his thoughts and words. And his goal was to prove to Theophilus that the things he was learning about Jesus were true!

Those who are Brains tend to do well when it comes to laying out well-reasoned arguments for Christianity. They present the gospel message in an intellectually stimulating and logical way. Their weakness? They can tend to come off as cold and uncaring.

Just because you get good grades doesn't mean you are a Brain in this sense. Being a Brain is more of a personality type than it is an IQ test.

DISCOVERING YOUR STYLE

So how do you discover your personal sharing style?

First of all pray and ask God to give you wisdom to discern it. Remember the promise of James 1:5, "If any of you lacks wisdom, he should ask God, who gives generously to all without finding fault, and it will be given to him."

Secondly, your initial "gut instinct" is probably right. When you read the descriptions of the Talker, Stalker, Buddy, and Brain, which one did you initially think best matched you? Your first impression when it comes to things like this is usually right!

Finally, I developed a little nonscientific "test" to help you identify your personal style of sharing Jesus. Circle the answer that applies *most* to you:

1. Which word describes you the most?
    A. Funny
    B. Bold
    ⌐ C. Caring
    D. Logical

2. "Sometimes I tend to . . .
    A. joke around too much."
    B. hurt people's feelings with my directness."
    ⌐ C. worry about what other people think of me."
    D. get frustrated with others who don't 'get it' when it comes to thought problems and mental challenges."

3. Your friends would probably describe you as . . .
    A. the life of the party.
    B. the leader of the pack.
    ⌐ C. a friend who really listens.
    D. the smart kid.

4. If you had a friend you wanted to lead to Christ, which of the following things would you be more likely to do?
    A. Find the most creative way (using humor if possible) you could possibly use to bring up the gospel message.

B. Just bring it up to him or her with a direct question.

C. Take your friend to the video arcade and pray that it naturally comes up in the conversation.

D. Give your friend a book or send him or her to a Web site that makes a strong, logical case for Christianity, and then talk about it afterward.

5. What makes you the most uncomfortable in a situation where you have the opportunity to share your faith?
   A. Not being able to bring it up in a natural and witty way.
   B. Beating around the bush.
   C. Making the other person feel uncomfortable.
   D. Not having the answers if they ask hard questions.

6. How would you bring up the gospel with total strangers?
   A. Get them laughing, get them talking, and then switch gears to Jesus naturally.
   B. Ask them if they know for sure they are going to heaven when they die.
   C. Try to talk to them and wait to see if they want to talk at all.
   D. Ask them questions about who they think Jesus was and if they are open to proof that He was the Son of God.

7. Which phrase below bests describes your style of sharing?
   A. Hey, bro! Listen to this!
   B. Are you talking to me? Good, 'cause I wanna talk to you!
   C. God gave us two ears and one mouth for a reason . . . to listen first!
   D. Resistance to my brain power is futile!

8. "I tend to get in trouble for . . .
     A. too much joking."
     B. being too blunt."
   —C. not much."
     D. arguing."

9. "If I were trying to motivate other Christians to share their
   faith, I would try to . . .
     A. talk them into it."
     B. take them out and do it with them."
     C. encourage them to build strong relationships with the
        lost first."
     D. teach them apologetics" (the art of "proving" Chris-
        tianity through historical, scientific, or archeological
        facts, fulfilled prophecy, etc.).

Add up your score here:
Number of A's ___, B's___, C's___, D's ____.

If you are mostly A's then you may be a Talker—funny, creative, and "the life of the party" when it comes to sharing Jesus.

If you are mostly B's then you may be a "Stalker"—direct,
bold, and "the leader of the pack" when it comes to sharing your
faith.

Scored mostly C's? Then you may be a Buddy—relational,
kind, and a true friend when it comes to telling others about
Jesus.

And if you marked mostly D's then you may be a Brain—
smart, logical, and a person who can make a strong case for Christianity with your sheer logic.

WHICH STYLE DID JESUS USE?

Jesus shows us the ultimate balance of all four sharing styles! We see Him being a Talker throughout the synoptic gospels (Matthew, Mark, and Luke) as He uses short, fictional stories called "parables" to share His message in creative, thought-provoking, and sometimes funny ways. We see Him being a "Stalker" in Matthew 23 when He takes on the religious leaders boldly in the temple and challenges their belief system and behavior without flinching. We see Jesus being a Buddy in John 4 when He broke cultural taboos to talk to a Samaritan woman, treat her with dignity and respect, and share with her the "living water" (aka "the gospel"). Finally we see Jesus as a Brain in Luke 24 when, after His resurrection, He used passages in the Old Testament to prove that He had to die and rise again from the dead.

As you can see from the graph on the next page, the four sharing styles are centered on Jesus! He is the ultimate balance that you should be seeking to achieve when it comes to sharing His message. What does this mean for you as you recognize your sharing style? Three things:

1. Keep your eyes on Jesus!

As you grow and mature in Christ you will find yourself "spilling over" into other styles. When I first started sharing my faith as a Talker/Stalker mix, I thought that my style was the best. But as I've kept my eyes on Jesus over the years, I've become more balanced—hopefully more like Jesus—as I've shared my faith.

2. Maximize your strengths and minimize your weaknesses!

Every style has built-in strengths and weaknesses. Whether you are bold, funny, relational, or logical, use it! Just realize your built-in weaknesses and minimize them as much as possible!

3. Learn to use different styles in different situations!

If you are a Buddy and you are standing at a bus stop with a complete stranger, you don't have time to build a friendship. Venture out and do what a Talker would do: Try to bring up the

Everybody has a unique sharing style!

TALKER

Description: Creative, funny, shares the gospel in persuasive ways, inspiring

Strengths: Articulate, persuasive

Weakness: Afraid to offend

Biblical Example: Philip

STALKER

Description: Direct, blunt, strong, shares the gospel in powerful and thought-provoking ways

Strengths: Bold, courageous, consistent

Weakness: Can turn people off

Biblical Example: Paul

BRAIN

Description: Smart and organized, shares the gospel in intellectually stimulating ways

Strengths: Logical

Weakness: Can be non-emotional and cold

Biblical Example: Luke

BUDDY

Description: Relational, loves to listen and serve, shares the gospel in compassionate ways

Strengths: Loves and listens

Weakness: May be afraid to bring it up

Biblical Example: Barnabas

gospel in a funny or creative way! If you are a Stalker and you just became part of the basketball team, try not giving the gospel in the first team huddle. You have all season long. Try being a Buddy/Stalker mix. Aggressively pursue one-on-one opportunities to build relationships and then bring it up!

A FINAL THOUGHT

Although the Bible doesn't flatly state that there are different styles of sharing the gospel, these styles are clearly seen throughout the New Testament. No one style is better than another. As a matter of fact, ultimately, the sharing style you have is not the most important issue. The most important thing is that you are lovingly communicating the gospel message in the power of the Spirit for the glory of God.

But now the question is, how do you get started sharing the gospel with your friends? How do you bring it up without throwing up?

CAN I GET A WITNESS?

I'm Rachael, 17, from Aurora, Colorado. I'm mostly a "Brain." I find ways to relate God to things I learn at school, like when we read Dante's Inferno or when we studied the Reformation. It's kind of like what Paul did with the people in Athens who had an altar "to an unknown God." Other people are more like Peter, getting in front of a crowd and giving them the message bluntly. God blesses both approaches.

SHARE

HOW

TO

SHARE

YOUR

FAITH

PART TWO

CHAPTER 7

HOW TO BRING IT UP WITHOUT THROWING UP

You are sitting across from your friend in the school cafeteria. Nobody else is at your table. The conversation "tone" is perfect. You are both talking in that strange friend zone where you know that you can bring up any subject and talk about it. You have been waiting and praying for the opportunity to tell your friend about Jesus and here it is. So what do you do? How do you bring Him up without throwing up?

There is no easy answer to this question. Why? Not because there's no simple way to introduce the gospel, but because there are a thousand ways to get the conversation started. But before we talk about those ways, there is one key principle you should understand: The toughest part of sharing your faith is not explaining the gospel, nor is it defending your faith. The toughest part is bringing it up the very first time.

In some ways my challenge to you is to just go for it. Don't hold back. Just push the words out of your mouth to trigger the conversation. After that it will be a whole lot easier to talk about heaven, hell, life, purpose, Jesus, sin, and hope. In this "game" the toughest part is the kickoff, the opening pitch, the starter's gun, or whatever sports analogy you want to mix in here.

Even the great apostle Paul struggled with this from time to time. Check out his request to the Ephesian believers: "Pray also for me, that whenever I open my mouth, words may be given me so that I will fearlessly make known the mystery of the gospel" (Ephesians 6:19). Paul wanted God to give him the right words to say as he brought up the gospel message to those he encountered. If the super apostle struggled at times bringing it up, don't feel bad if you do too!

So how do you get the conversation with your friends (or with strangers for that matter) started? Well, it depends on a lot of things. It depends on the situation, their interests and ideas, how much time you have to spend talking, etc. One of the key things it depends on is your own style of sharing your faith.

OPENING QUESTIONS

If you are a Talker (creative, funny, persuasive) then some opening questions you may feel more comfortable using include the following:

- What is most important to you in life?
- How would you rate your interest in spiritual things on a scale from 1 to 10? Why?
- Would you mind if I shared with you what I'm most passionate about?

If you're a Stalker (direct, bold, relentless) then some opening questions you may feel more comfortable using could be:

- Do you know for sure that you are going to heaven when you die?
- If I could tell you how you could know, would that be good news?
- Do you think you are good enough to make it to heaven?

If you're a Buddy (relational, loving, kind) then your opening questions could be:

- Would you tell me about your spiritual journey so far?
- Would you mind telling me about yourself and what is important to you?
- Can you share with me your view of God?

If you're a Brain (logical, smart, convincing) then you could ask:

- Who do you think Jesus was—God Himself, a good teacher, or something else?
- Would it surprise you to know that there are hundreds of prophecies about Christ in the Old Testament that were fulfilled with amazing precision?
- What do you believe about God and why?

These are just samples and examples of opening questions you could use, depending on your primary style of sharing your faith. There is no perfect list because there are no perfect questions. In other words, there is no way to avoid the uncomfortable first step of "bringing it up" with a friend, classmate, teammate, stranger, or family member. These questions give you something to start with, but sharing Jesus with somebody still makes your palms sweat and your heartbeat accelerate.

But fear can be useful if it reminds you to pray, because when you pray, you get back in the "power zone" of being controlled by

God's Spirit. It's only when we are Spirit-Charged Super Saints that we can be fully used by God to advance the kingdom of God in power!

SALVATION SEGUES

The dictionary definition of "segue" is "to move smoothly and unhesitatingly from one state, condition, situation, or element to another."[1]

When it comes to sharing Jesus, we must learn to move from one subject of conversation to the subject of God, sin, and salvation in a smooth and natural way. This is more of an art that is learned than a science that can be taught. We learn it by watching how the best of the best did it in the pages of Scripture. Who is the best? Jesus, of course! Check out where He graciously and skillfully makes a salvation segue from a cup of water to the spiritual realm in John 4:6-14:

> Jesus, tired as he was from the journey, sat down by [Jacob's] well. It was about the sixth hour.
>
> When a Samaritan woman came to draw water, Jesus said to her, "Will you give me a drink?" (His disciples had gone into the town to buy food.)
>
> The Samaritan woman said to him, "You are a Jew and I am a Samaritan woman. How can you ask me for a drink?" (For Jews do not associate with Samaritans.)
>
> Jesus answered her, "If you knew the gift of God and who it is that asks you for a drink, you would have asked him and he would have given you living water."

"Sir," the woman said, "you have nothing to draw with and the well is deep. Where can you get this living water? Are you greater than our father Jacob, who gave us the well and drank from it himself, as did also his sons and his flocks and herds?"

Jesus answered, "Everyone who drinks this water will be thirsty again, but whoever drinks the water I give him will never thirst. Indeed, the water I give him will become in him a spring of water welling up to eternal life."

As we've already seen, Jesus was breaking cultural taboos even talking with this Samaritan woman, but He did it anyway. He loved her and wanted her to know the joy of the forgiveness that He had to offer.

When she was talking about water in the liquid form, Jesus was talking about spiritual water. Just as a cold drink of water can satisfy your thirst on a hot day, Jesus can satisfy your soul in a world of pain and disappointment. The difference is that with Jesus, once you drink of Him, you will never thirst again for any-

CAN I GET A WITNESS?

I'm Jim. I'm 15, from Lawrenceville, Georgia. Here's the thing man, no matter how much we are scared, God is always with us. Why should we be scared someone is going to make fun of us when we know that the Lord our God is there always? Who cares what other people say about you? What matters is that you know that God is always with you, no matter what, and that you took a stand for your beliefs.

thing else. Contrary to some Gatorade commercials you may see, Jesus is the ultimate thirst quencher.

As you keep your eyes on Jesus, staying filled with His Spirit and alert to the everyday opportunities that God has granted, you too can learn to use salvation segues to take an everyday subject and turn it toward something spiritual.

So how do you learn to use salvation segues more and more? Here are a few hints:

Pray for Open Eyes to See the Opportunities Every Day

Right after Jesus shared the "living water" with the woman at the well, the disciples came and wondered what was going on. Jesus told them to open their spiritual eyes to see the people all around them who desperately needed to hear and believe the gospel. Using another analogy, Jesus rebukes them in John 4:35 by commanding them, "Open your eyes and look at the fields! They are ripe for harvest."

Jesus wants you to be aware of those all around you every

CAN I GET A WITNESS?

My name is Melody. I am 14 and I live in Kansas City, Kansas. I've been talking to one of my friends about church and stuff and trying to tell her about Christ through two bands: P.O.D. and Switchfoot. She is going through struggles with her parents and cutting, and she really wants someone to talk to. I've been praying for her and brought her to church once and have been trying to use music to talk about my faith.

single day who are spiritually ripe and ready. Pray for open eyes to see the opportunities that are already there at school, work, home, and play.

Look for "The Fork in the Road"

While you are in conversation, look for what I call "the fork in the road." What is that? It's the point in the conversation where you can turn it one direction or the other. You can turn down the highway of everyday banter about life, sports, movies, music, friends, blah, blah, blah. Or you can take the turn at the fork in the road toward more spiritual subjects.

For instance, let's say you are talking to a friend about a teacher. Maybe this is your favorite teacher. She always has a great attitude and is willing to serve. Then you suddenly remember that she is a Christian. You can take the highway of everyday blah, blah, blah, or you can take the turn toward the more awkward by saying something like, "Maybe one of the reasons she has such a good attitude is because she is in tune with God on a deeper level." From there you can continue down the road of spiritual discussion to the point where you are listening to your friend's spiritual beliefs and sharing yours.

WARNING!

Be careful with your salvation segues! Try to make them as smooth as possible, not forced. For instance, if somebody says to you, "It's sure hot in here," don't say, "It's hot in hell, too!" Be as sensitive and smooth as possible when you make a transition from your everyday conversation to eternal matters.

Here is a list of conversation subjects and examples of how you can take the turn at the fork in the road to make your salvation segue:

Them:	You:
"I really liked that movie. It was awesome!"	"Me too! Did you notice the spiritual analogies that were everywhere?"
"I just lost my aunt to cancer."	"I'm sorry. It makes you think about your mortality and what happens after you die, doesn't it?"
(Girls) "Why don't you ever wear that shirt I got you?"	"Nothing personal. It's a cool shirt. But because of my convictions I choose not to wear stuff that is too revealing."
(Guys) "How much do you bench-press?"	"Two-fifty. But to me there is a whole lot of stuff more important than how much you bench."
"I love that song!"	"Yeah, it rocks! There's another song on that CD that talks about how much they hate religion. I like that song because, to me, it's not about religion. It's about a relationship with God."
"I hate my dad! He's only into himself."	"I'm so sorry. I guess that's why I'm so thankful for my dad . . . not my earthly father, but my heavenly one."

On and on the list goes. As a matter of fact, I'm convinced that any conversation, anytime, can eventually be segued to the subject of salvation. Just be aware and look for the fork in the road.

WHEN IN DOUBT, GO FOR IT IN LOVE ANYWAY!

Okay, let's say that you are in the midst of a conversation waiting for that fork in the road to appear. It doesn't. What do you do? Do you wait for another day and another conversation? Or do you just go for it?

Of course you must be sensitive to the Holy Spirit's leading. But to be honest, how often is the Spirit going to guide you to keep your mouth shut?

Sometimes we can't make a natural and smooth turn toward spiritual subjects. In those times I encourage you to go for it anyway. How? Ditch the salvation segue approach and simply say something like, "Would you mind if I changed the subject?"

Subjects change all the time in the natural ebb and flow of teen conversations anyway. Once you change the subject, just

If you are in a small group of Christian teenagers, you can all "practice" making salvation segues by doing a little game that I used to play when I was a teenager. Somebody would pick a subject, any subject, and the first person to make the most natural segue toward the subject of salvation wins. A ketchup bottle, a football game, a diamond ring, or a big, steaming pile of manure all can be used as subjects. Believe it or not, this little, goofy game will sharpen your abilities to make salvation segues every day!

bring it up. You can use whatever question you feel comfortable using according to your style of sharing the gospel or you can just start talking about it.

Obviously, this is not the ideal scenario. But sometimes you've just got to bring it up. When you do, remember this verse in 1 Peter 4:8: "Above all, love each other deeply, because love covers over a multitude of sins." As long as you transition toward the gospel in love—awkward, smooth, or otherwise—people will usually cut you slack.

Memorize some questions that you feel comfortable using to bring up spiritual subjects, pray for open eyes to see the opportunities all around you every day, look for the most natural "fork in the road," and when all else fails just bring it up in love.

But after you bring it up, you'd better be sure you know what to say next. You'd better be equipped to take your friends on the GOSPEL Journey.

NOTE: The GOSPEL Journey acronym was developed by Dare 2 Share Ministries to explain the key points of the gospel message as they span the whole story of the Bible from Genesis to Revelation.

CHAPTER 8

UNDERSTANDING THE GOSPEL JOURNEY

Have you ever been on a backpacking trip in the mountains? Being from Colorado, I've had the privilege of traversing the beautiful, rugged, and sometimes dangerous Rocky Mountains from time to time.

Experienced backpackers and rock climbers know that you enter these mountains with a mixture of fear and excitement. Take them too lightly and you could end up neck deep in an avalanche or as a puddle of gush at the bottom of a cliff.

In a lot of ways sharing the gospel with somebody is like taking them on a journey to the crest of a distant mountain. The top of the mountain is heaven. The problem is that between you and your final destination lie many dangers, the biggest of which is a huge, seemingly unbridgeable chasm. If you can get your friend across this Grand Canyon-sized hole in the earth, then their salvation is secure. If you can't, then he or she will never experience the view from the top of the mountain on the other side of the chasm.

God has equipped you with a backpack filled with everything you need to take your friend on this exciting and exhausting journey. Your compass is the Holy Spirit. Your map is the Word of God. And you are the guide.

Your goal is to help your friend find a way across this gigantic chasm to God. The challenge is that there is only one way across. Jesus claimed to be "the way and the truth and the life." He is the only way across and you must help your friend find Him if you are to succeed in this adventure.

The challenge is this: How do you convince your friend to take the journey in the first place? This becomes especially tricky when you consider that your friend may already be way off course or on a different pathway altogether. If your friend is steeped in Mormonism or Islam, for example, there is a good chance that he or she is way down the wrong road, headed toward the wrong destination.

You may have some friends who are well on their way down the path toward eternal life but have stalled out for some reason. For instance, if your friend was raised in a solid church that preached the gospel, yet for some reason or another has never trusted in Christ, he or she may be stalled out somewhere along the way to trusting in Jesus. Perhaps all your friend needs is a little nudge from you to continue the journey.

All of your friends, classmates, and teammates, even the atheist ones, are on a spiritual journey toward somewhere. The question is, how do we get them on the one path that leads to eternal life? How do we get them across the chasm and on their way toward heaven?

A JOURNEY I'LL NEVER FORGET

Last summer I took the journey of a lifetime with a group of teenagers whom I had never met before. There was Andy the atheist jock who loved to discuss why he didn't believe in the existence of God. There was Ashley the ex-Jehovah's Witness who had many questions about the whole gospel message. There was Tasondra the city girl, Eric the Episcopalian, Ben the Presbyterian, and Tiffany the minister's daughter. One of the more colorful characters was Stephén. He was a Cajun Wiccan teenager who carried a chip on his shoulder and had a smart-aleck comment for everyone about everything.

I took these seven very diverse kids on a six-day adventure in the Colorado mountains for a kind of *Survivor*-type experience. While my friend Zane guided them through the mountain adventures (rock climbing, white-water rafting, rappelling), I guided them through the story of the gospel as it unfolded throughout the Bible.

We used a simple acrostic as our road map through the biblical truths. And, you guessed right, it spelled out the word "GOSPEL."

Starting in Genesis, I shared with them the six key truths of the gospel story through six key phrases. Here they are:

God created us to be with Him. (Genesis 1, 2)
Our sins separate us from God. (Genesis 3)
Sins cannot be removed by good deeds. (Genesis 4–Malachi)
Paying the price for sin, Jesus died and rose again.
    (Matthew–Luke)
Everyone who trusts in Him alone has eternal life.
    (John–Jude)
Life that's eternal means we will be with Him forever.
    (Revelation)

Every day we did some kind of new and exciting challenge, and we tied that day's adventure into one of the sessions for the day. For instance, after a get-to-know-you hike high above the continental divide, I talked about G—the fact that God created us to be with Him. In this session I shared what the Word of God said about who we are and how we got here. By using the story of the creation account in Genesis chapters 1–2, I painted a picture of God's original intent for humankind before Satan slithered in and it all came crashing down in Genesis 3. In this first session I talked about the doctrine of the Trinity, creation versus evolution, the image of God in people, and more. I then opened it up for questions, arguments, and discussions . . . and got more than I bargained for!

The next five points covered the rest of the gospel story as it unfolds throughout the rest of the Bible. We talked through the Ten Commandments, the sacrificial system outlined in the Old Testament, the birth of Christ, and much more. These teenagers never once seemed to get bored. Although we were covering full-out theology disguised as core issues of life (relationships, purpose, sin, forgiveness, redemption, and hope), they were fully engaged. It didn't hurt that we were able to use powerful visual illustrations like the continental divide, a sheer rock wall, or a ropes course to make our points.

What happened over the course of six days amazed me. The intense discussions spilled over into the SUV rides, the rafting trip, and the hot tub!

Three of the kids who came with us were already Christians when they began the journey. I had the privilege of helping two of the remaining four students across the chasm into a personal relationship with Jesus Christ. Being a part of their journey to Jesus was one of the most spiritually rewarding experiences I have ever had!

And you can take your friends on the GOSPEL Journey, too. You can take them on the journey to the spiritual mountain of salvation through Jesus by understanding, memorizing, and mastering the six parts of this message yourself and then unfolding this powerful message to them in a relevant and loving way.

Over the next six short chapters, let me continue the backpacking analogy and be your guide through the GOSPEL Journey.

NOTE: This unscripted Rocky Mountain adventure was captured on film and developed into a reality series. Available through Dare 2 Share Ministries, the GOSPEL Journey Adventure Kit is designed to be used as an evangelism training tool for Christian teens and an evangelistic outreach tool for non-Christian teens. The students' unforgettable quest to understand the gospel message straight from the pages of Scripture unfolds with raw, real, and riveting discussions.

CHAPTER 9

GOD CREATED US TO BE WITH HIM

Our trip starts out on a beautiful day. The trek we take up the steep mountain path is laced with flowers and takes us through dense forests. Lush plants and trees line both sides of the narrow walkway. The sound of chirping birds, buzzing bees, and ribbiting frogs fills the forest around us. This teeming jungle in the mountains is alive with life in all shapes and sizes. So far so good.

◆ ◆ ◆

THE FIRST GARDEN

In some ways that's probably what Adam and Eve experienced in the Garden of Eden so many years ago. They were surrounded by sheer beauty, which was unscathed by the ravages of sin. They too were on a journey, not an earthy path through the jungle, but a spiritual quest to please God in this brand-new adventure called "life." And speaking of life, it was teeming all around and above them.

God had created pristine lakes, vast oceans, never-ending forests, and a shockingly beautiful garden setting for Adam and

Eve to enjoy. The sun shone its warm rays on their naked skin at just the right temperature. It never got too hot in the daytime. It never got too cold at night. The food was great. The animals were tame. Everything was, well, perfect.

"Then God said, 'Let us make man in our image, in our likeness . . .'" (Genesis 1:26).

All the animals that stomped on the earth God had spoken into existence. He simply uttered, "Let there be . . ." and there was.

But He took His time with Adam. He found a puddle of mud in the Garden of Eden and knelt down into it. He began scooping it together and working it with His fingers until a form started taking shape. What a sight that must have been, the God of the universe covered in mud as He crafted the first man out of dirt, dust, and cool jungle water.

God formed Adam from the mud and breathed into this sculpture's nostrils the breath of life. The statue blinked, then yawned, stretched, and stood. The mud became blood . . . and flesh and bone and muscle.

Adam was in the ultimate setting. He had it all: perfect fellowship with his Creator, the perfect setting in a weed-free garden full of lush beauty. And God had big plans for Adam—organize the garden, name all the animals, and rule over the earth and over every animal, fish, bug, and plant.

Only one thing was missing.

Adam looked around and saw Mr. and Mrs. Ape, Mr. and Mrs. Ferret, and Mr. and Mrs. Hippopotamus. All around him he saw couples. But there was nobody for him. Nobody. For the first time he had a sense of profound loneliness. As Genesis 2:20 says, "For Adam no suitable helper was found."

God wasted no time fixing that problem. This is what the book of Genesis says about it:

> Then God said, "Let us make man in our image, in our likeness, and let them rule over the fish of the sea and the birds of the air, over the livestock, over all the earth, and over all the creatures that move along the ground." (1:26)
>
> So the LORD God caused the man to fall into a deep sleep; and while he was sleeping, he took one of the man's ribs and closed up the place with flesh. Then the LORD God made a woman from the rib he had taken out of the man, and he brought her to the man.
>
> The man said,
> "This is now bone of my bones
> and flesh of my flesh;
> she shall be called 'woman,'
> for she was taken out of man."
>
> For this reason a man will leave his father and mother and be united to his wife, and they will become one flesh.
>
> The man and his wife were both naked, and they felt no shame. (2:21-25)

Adam and Eve were open, honest, innocent, and as naked as jaybirds. *(How did that expression start anyway? Come on, isn't a jaybird as naked as other birds out there? Don't feathers count as clothes? But I digress.)*

These two sin-free beings experienced everything God originally intended for all mankind to experience. They had no fights, no disagreements, only love, peace, and absolute harmony. They found significance in the tending of the garden. They found security in a strong relationship with God and with each other. It was truly paradise on earth.

GOOD NEWS, BAD NEWS

The good news is that God's original plan was that all humanity would be happy, healthy, and holy, in perfect relationship with their Creator. The bad news (which we see in the next chapter) is that the whole deal got messed up by sin. As a result there are death, sin, war, crime, broken relationships, busted dreams, and depression in the world.

Most people don't know that God created them so that He could pour His love out on them. Adam and Eve had everything our world is looking and longing for so badly. Physically, emotionally, spiritually, and socially they were completely fulfilled.

Stop and think of what your friends are looking for in life. Adam and Eve had it all.

Many people today are on a quest for physical fitness. Adam was so healthy that even after he was condemned to die, he still lived hundreds of years (Genesis 5:4).

People want vocational fulfillment. Adam and Eve had that. God gave them three jobs to do. They were to take care of the Garden of Eden (Genesis 2:15), rule over the animal kingdom, and fill the earth with their children and their children's children (Genesis 1:28).

They want emotional fulfillment. Adam and Eve had pure, unblushing emotional fulfillment. Nude wasn't crude in the Garden of Eden. It was a sign of transparency, honesty, and purity.

They want sex. Adam and Eve had it. It was God-sanctioned, unbridled, unhindered passion.

They want wealth and power. Adam and Eve had power over the entire world and everything in it. Has anyone else in history even come close to that?

Spiritually Adam and Eve walked with God, they talked with God, and they were with God. He was not hiding behind a veil in a temple or a cloud on a mountain or a burning bush to shield His glory from frail humanity. He was with them. They didn't shrink in

TASONDRA'S EYES OPEN

I wish you could have seen Tasondra's eyes when she saw the beauty of the continental divide in the Rocky Mountains from the top of a huge mountain. I think it was her first time above timberline (so high that trees don't grow there). This city girl understood all about magnificent buildings and the complexities of living in the city. But to experience the rush and thrill of the majestic views toward the top of a Colorado peak left her speechless and breathless (the air is much thinner 13,000 feet up!). It was as if she were the first person to ever behold God's creation—a new Eve, if you will, dumb-struck by the beauty of the garden. The moment was broken, however, when a group of mountain bikers pedaled up and stopped to catch their breath. She was suddenly snapped back to her quick-witted, funny, city-girl self. But still, Tasondra's heart had sensed the call of creation, and it struck a chord in her soul. That momentary peace she had felt was meant to last forever. God's original intention had been so good.

terror from His glorious presence because they had no reason to run. They literally hung out with God, like you do with your friends after school.

Aren't all these things what the typical person today is looking for? Physical health, wealth and power, emotional, vocational, relational, and spiritual fulfillment. Yes, Adam and Eve had it all.

Then sin came walking in and everything got twisted.

On this first stage of our journey up the mountain, the sky overhead is an intense, breathtaking, brilliant blue. Sunlight filters through the trees, giving the lush forest around us a fresh, sparkling appearance. The patches of shade are cool and refreshing. We feel safe, secure, and satisfied. But off in the distance beyond our field of vision, dark clouds are gathering that will wreak havoc on our perfect surroundings. A storm is brewing that will soon soak the terrain with pain, shame, and sin.

CHAPTER 10

OUR SINS SEPARATE US FROM GOD

As we continue on the beautiful path filled with the luscious plants of God's love, weeds start to sprout before our eyes. For the first time we see a dead carcass of some animal by the pathway. It reeks of death—new death—death that was earned by the sin of Adam and Eve.

A storm begins to gather as we approach a huge cliff. The chasm wasn't there before, and the horizon looks strange and eerie now. We tremble when we realize the cliff cuts off our path to eternal life. Across the deep, dark, fog-filled valley beneath us we can barely see the continuation of the path on the other side. It looks like it's a mile or so away. There's no way we can get from here to there.

The whole thing looks like a huge chunk of earth has dropped off into the abyss. What's left is an uncrossable chasm that the strongest arm in football couldn't throw across on his best day.

◆ ◆ ◆

THE CONSEQUENCES OF THE FIRST SIN

The chasm was created when Adam and Eve sinned. On one side of the chasm are sin, death, and hopelessness. On the other side is eternal life. This huge, gaping, Grand Canyon-sized hole represents the separation that began when Adam and Eve sinned for the first time.

Adam and Eve knew and enjoyed the presence and purity of God in the Garden of Eden. When they chose to sin (by eating the forbidden fruit) a chasm was created. This hole can't be filled. It's much too big. It can't be crossed. It's far too wide. It represents the immeasurable distance between a holy, sinless God and a selfish, sinful humanity.

When Adam and Eve ate of the forbidden fruit, something deadly took place inside the inner caverns of their souls. They were corrupted. They became depraved. The cancer of selfishness and disease of pride spread throughout every fiber of their spiritual beings. Once destined to rule the earth, they now became slaves to sin and Satan.

What was their first reaction after disobeying God?

To cover their shame!

Genesis 3:7 explains the sad aftermath of their sinful choices: "Then the eyes of both of them were opened, and they realized they were naked; so they sewed fig leaves together and made coverings for themselves."

Their second reaction?

To hide from God!

Genesis 3:8-9 puts it this way: "Then the man and his wife heard the sound of the LORD God as he was walking in the garden in the cool of the day, and they hid from the LORD God among the trees of the garden. But the LORD God called to the man, 'Where are you?'"

The rest of the Bible describes a cosmic hide-and-seek game where God searches for us, for humanity, but we are still hiding in the gardens of religion, philosophy, materialism, or hedonism. Yet God has never stopped calling out "Where are you?" to a lost, depraved, and hiding world.

Adam and Eve's third reaction?

To play the blame game!

Man blames the woman. Woman blames the serpent. By this

STEPHÉN, MY WILD, WICCAN FRIEND

Of all the participants of the GOSPEL Journey, Stephén was the wildest, proudest, and loudest. He attacked every day with a smile and a determination to win whatever competition we would have that day.

During the teaching times he would ask a lot of questions and make a lot of comments, almost to the point of dominating the Q&A time. At first many of the other participants were irritated by him. But Stephén grew on everybody. He was a nice kid with a small frame, a big mouth—and a big heart to match!

During one of the teaching times, I had everybody take a mirror and look into it for 10 seconds. I asked everyone to think of one thing they had done in the last 12 months that they were ashamed of, that God was ashamed of. When I asked at the end of this experience how it had made them feel, Stephén was completely honest and vulnerable. He shared how guilty he felt, how much he sensed that he was an absolute sinner in that moment. Now, you have to understand, this was significant—Wiccans don't really believe in sin. But in that moment Stephén did. My loud, proud little friend got quiet, and I think he heard the footsteps of God coming in the distance.

time the whole of paradise had unraveled irreparably. Sin was at the root of all of this tragedy. What was the end result of this one sinful choice? Broken relationships, busted dreams, shattered lives, and death.

Believe it or not, Adam's sin is the reason corruption, famine, crime, and war steal the newspaper headlines. Scripture tells us in Romans 5:12, "Therefore, just as sin entered the world through one man, and death through sin, and in this way death came to all men, because all sinned—"

Adam was mankind's spiritual representative before God. When he sinned, he sinned on our behalf. If the President declares war on some country then we, as Americans, declare war as well. The President is our political representative and acts on our behalf whether we like it or not.

The same is true of Adam. When he declared war on God through his singular act of rebellion, he was acting as our spiritual representative. As a result, whether we like it or not, all of us declared war on God as well.

Through Adam's defiance of God's one simple command, the floodgates of sin were opened. As a result, from the womb to the tomb we are soaked in sin. It drenches our thoughts and motives. It seeps through our words and actions. It drowns our lives and relationships.

This sin nature can also be compared to cancer. It corrupted the very DNA of our souls. Adam's sin spread like a genetic defect to every one of his children and their children's children until it made its way to you and me.

When explaining the gospel to someone, it is important to explain the relationship that God created mankind to enjoy with Him and how sin ruined that beautiful unity. Since the day that

Eve gave birth to Cain, mankind has been born kicking and screaming, selfish and sinful, mutinous and murderous. It's in our blood. We have all fallen from the dysfunctional family tree called depravity.

FIRE AND BRIMSTONE

The ultimate consequence of this separation from God is eternal separation from Him in a literal place called hell. Perhaps the saddest and scariest phrase in Scripture is 2 Thessalonians 1:7-9: "[Jesus will appear] in blazing fire with his powerful angels. He will punish those who do not know God and do not obey the gospel of our Lord Jesus. They will be punished with everlasting destruction and shut out from the presence of the Lord and from the majesty of his power."

Think about those words "shut out from the presence of the Lord." The scariest thing about hell is not the presence of darkness or flame or pain but the absence of hope and love and Jesus. If this doesn't break your heart for the lost, check your pulse, because you might be dead.

Hell is scary. It represents something even more intimidating than fire and flame. It stands for God's hatred for sin. Hell burns forever because God's hatred of wickedness burns forever. It takes an eternity of flame to quench God's holy disdain of that which is evil.

It is vital that we help our friends who don't know Christ realize that the relationship God wanted to enjoy with all of us in Genesis 1 was completely ruined by sin in Genesis 3. When sin came walking in, communion with God went running out.

And there's nothing you can do about that.

◆ ◆ ◆

So here we are, stuck on one side of the valley of the shadow of death created by Adam and Eve's sinful choice. A cold, harsh wind whips about us. We pull out our rain gear, and suddenly the storm clouds unleash their torrents. But our gear is inadequate to protect us from the fury of the storm and we are soon drenched and shivering. In our misery and despair we realize that if we are to continue the GOSPEL Journey, we have to find a way across the gaping chasm.

CHAPTER 11

SINS CANNOT BE REMOVED BY GOOD DEEDS

This fog-filled hole looming before us presents a big problem. We start to strategize how we can get across and continue our journey. We think, Well, I'm a pretty good distance jumper. Maybe if I got a running start . . . then we look across the gargantuan chasm and think again.

Maybe I can attach a rope to a spear of some kind and drive it into a tree or something on the other side. It could be the beginning of a bridge of some sort.

But down deep inside we finally come to the grim realization there is no way to cross it on our own. We can't make it.

ON THE WRONG SIDE OF THE CHASM

This is the same realization every person must have when it comes to gaining eternal life. More often than not, people think they can cross the chasm of sin by being a good person. Take a survey among your classmates and you may be surprised. Just ask them one simple question: "What does it take to get to heaven?" You'll probably get answers that include the following:

"I think I'm a pretty good person."

"I try to live by the Ten Commandments."

"I have been going to church all of my life."

"I have never killed anybody or anything like that."

Most teenagers think that if they live a good life and are a nice person, then those behaviors in some way will get them across to heaven. They are steeped in a good-works mentality that says you can earn your way into heaven through acts of religious devotion or social justice, or even by being a halfway decent human being.

There are at least two big problems with this line of thinking.

Big Problem No. 1:
One sin is enough to condemn you to hell

Think about it. Unless you live a perfect, totally sinless life, you can not enter the presence of a perfect, holy God. James 2:10 puts it this way: "For whoever keeps the whole law and yet stumbles at just one point is guilty of breaking all of it." In other words, the Ten Commandments are a package deal. You bust one, you've busted them all. Bottom line is that it's bad news for the human race.

From God's perspective a non-Christian is immersed in sin and living a life outside of relationship with Him. Romans 3:10-12 quotes the Old Testament and paints a bleak picture:

> "There is no one righteous, not even one;
> there is no one who understands,
> no one who seeks God.
> All have turned away,
> they have together become worthless;

there is no one who does good,
not even one."

The standard of getting into heaven is perfection—not just being good by the world's standards.

Big Problem No. 2:
Your good deeds can't make up for your bad ones

First, God sees to the core of every person's heart and knows that the motives behind our good deeds are never perfectly pure. God knows what we do and why we do it. Our good deeds may not be really so good. What look like good deeds on the outside can be springing forth from a heart filled with selfish, sinful motives.

Secondly, we can't work our way to heaven by doing more good than we do evil. From Genesis 4 all the way through the last chapter of the Bible, the Bible shows that our sins could never be removed by good deeds. Every person ever born (except Jesus) was conceived in sin and lives in sin. Ephesians 5:5 makes it clear that "no immoral, impure or greedy person . . . has any inheritance in the kingdom of Christ and of God."

We all lie. We all lust. We all hate. We all covet. We all miss the mark on a daily basis. Only those who are as righteous as the Father Himself can be a part of the celestial kingdom. That means we are stuck on the wrong side of the chasm, and in and of ourselves, there's not a thing we can do about it.

THE HAMMER AND THE HEALER

Sometimes you need to use the hammer of the law before you introduce somebody to the ultimate Healer of souls. What is the law? It's summed up in the Ten Commandments. These were the 10 nonnegotiables that God required of the Israelites (and of us!).

Here they are as listed in Exodus 20:3-17:

1. You shall have no other gods before me.

   Have you ever put somebody else before God?

◆

2. You shall not make for yourself an idol in the form of anything in heaven above or on the earth beneath or in the waters below.

   Have you ever put something else before God?

◆

3. You shall not misuse the name of the LORD your God.

   Have you ever used the name of God in vain by saying "God _____!" or "Jesus Christ!" or "God!" in anger?

◆

4. Remember the Sabbath day by keeping it holy.

   Do you take one day a week to rest and reflect on God?

◆

5. Honor your father and mother.

   Have you always honored the wishes of your parents with a good attitude? Uh oh!

◆

6. You shall not murder.

   Have you ever murdered somebody? Before you answer that, remember that the Bible says that if you hate somebody you've broken the spirit of this command (1 John 3:15). Oops!

◆

7. You shall not commit adultery.

    Have you sinned sexually with a member of the opposite or same sex? Remember that Jesus tells us in Matthew 5:28 that if we've lusted in our minds, we have broken this command in the eyes of God. Not good.

    ◆

8. You shall not steal.

    Have you ever stolen anything? What about time from your employer by surfing the Internet on company time? What about illegal downloading? What about stealing attention during class or stealing glory for somebody else's accomplishments?

    ◆

9. You shall not give false testimony against your neighbor.

    Have you ever lied about anything to anybody including exaggerations and "little white lies"?

    ◆

10. You shall not covet your neighbor's house. You shall not covet your neighbor's wife, or his manservant or maidservant, his ox or donkey, or anything that belongs to your neighbor.

    Have you ever coveted what somebody else had? Somebody's looks, strength, car, cash, girlfriend, or boyfriend?

If we're honest, we'd admit that we break most of these commands a lot of the time. The problem is this: To get into heaven trying to obey the Ten Commandments, we would have to obey all of them perfectly all of the time from the moment we were born until the second that we died!

Swinging the Hammer with Grace and Love

As you share your faith with your friends, you may find that some of them think they are already good enough to make it into heaven. If they do, just bust out this Ten Commandments test on them, and they'll soon discover that they are not.

Sometimes it is essential to break down people's sense of pride and self-confidence in their own goodness before they'll be receptive to Jesus. That's where the hammer comes in handy. A Christian must use it lovingly and skillfully to shatter their

---

ANDY . . . MY NICE NEMESIS

Out of all the students who participated in the GOSPEL Journey project, Andy challenged me the most. Don't get me wrong, he was a very nice young man. I guess because he was so athletic, I wasn't ready for a mind that was every bit as chiseled as his body. Andy was always the first to question what I was communicating from the Bible. He asked any question that a well-educated atheist adult twice his age would ask. But he asked each question with a tremendous respect.

One of the points Andy had the hardest time with was the Bible's contention that our sins cannot be removed by good deeds. If there was a heaven, he assumed it was for those who were good enough to enter, no matter what their religion. He talked to me several times about this problem that he just couldn't reconcile in his quick-witted mind.

Andy did well in all the *Survivor*-esque challenges because of his athleticism. But the best challenge was the one he gave me every time I shared the gospel message.

self-sufficiency until they recognize they are sinners who deserve the judgment of God. Make sure you admit you are a sinner too. Once they realize they aren't "good enough," we can then introduce them to the Healer of their souls, Jesus Christ Himself.

Just as we realize that we can never make it across the chasm through our own efforts, the raging storm begins to abate. The heavy clouds begin to break apart and the dense fog filling the abyss that blocks our path begins to lift. We can now vaguely make out a rope bridge that spans the huge chasm. We can't help but notice that this little, narrow bridge is drenched blood-red . . . and we wonder why.

CHAPTER 12

PAYING THE PRICE FOR SIN, JESUS DIED AND ROSE AGAIN

Intrigued, we make our way toward the mysterious rope bridge stretching across the massive chasm. Hope rises up inside us, but doubts creep into our minds as well. Is the bridge ahead an illusive mirage? If it is real, how did it get here? Why does it appear to be drenched in blood? Will it be sturdy enough to support us? The questions bombard us as we struggle to keep our footing on the wet, slippery pathway overlooking the chasm. We push back our fear and continue moving cautiously forward, seeking answers.

◆ ◆ ◆

THE GOD-MAN

Two thousand years ago in the small village of Bethlehem, God became the God-man. Fully God and fully man. Jesus was born the Son of God and the Son of Man. Absolute purity and love wrapped up in one awesome package.

He lived a perfect life, died a horrible death, and experienced a glorious resurrection. He did it all for one reason . . . to redeem us from the bonds of sin and Satan; to rescue us from hell and hopelessness.

Remember the big picture. God created us to be with Him. But we blew it. Our sins separated us from Him. But thank the Lord that is not where the story ends. God sent His own Son to bear the consequences of those countless sins on our behalf. He did it to rekindle that relationship with us once and for all.

His Horrible Death

Stop for a moment to contemplate the significance of Christ's death on our behalf. Matthew, Mark, and Luke describe the gruesome process that Jesus went through when He suffered for our sins.

After Jesus had been brutally beaten beyond recognition and mocked by a throng of Roman soldiers, He was nailed to a rough, wooden cross. As His body hung naked and twisted, bloodied and bruised for six long hours on the cross, suspended by three nails and His love for you and me, history was being changed forever. For on that cross Jesus was absorbing the judgment of the Father for the sinfulness of all humanity. That's why Jesus screamed in Aramaic, "My God, my God, why have you forsaken me?"

The pain reflected in His scream was not from the gaping wounds in His body but from the fierce, unseen scourge that tore His soul. When Jesus was hanging on the cross, God the Father turned His back on His Son while pouring out His judgment on Him for us.

In that one moment Jesus felt the sting of a trillion hells compressed into one finite moment. He absorbed in full measure the entirety of God's wrath toward the sins of all humanity, including any sin you and I ever committed.

Moments later He declared in triumph the three words of ultimate victory, "IT IS FINISHED!"

The transaction was complete. The price was paid. The sacrifice made. Your sins and mine were obliterated in one sweeping act of God's love and justice.

The Chronicles of Narnia

In the book and movie *The Lion, the Witch and the Wardrobe*, Edmund, the younger brother, makes a deal with the White Witch who rules Narnia, agreeing to betray his brother and sisters for a treat called Turkish Delight. As a result of his sinful choice, tragedy unfolds and the whole of Narnia is threatened with eternal winter under the White Witch's evil rule.

But the great lion Aslan makes the choice to die for Edmund's sin. According to the timeless and eternal laws of Narnia, if somebody sins, they must die for their own transgression, unless somebody innocent chooses to die for their sin instead. After Aslan's horrible death at the hands of the White Witch and her evil minions, Aslan rises from the dead to win the war and destroy the witch.

What a perfect picture of the gospel story! The true "Aslan" is Jesus Christ, the Lion of Judah. Edmund's sin represents Adam's choice to disobey God and betray the whole of humanity, not for a piece of Turkish Delight but for a piece of forbidden fruit. He and all of humanity are condemned to an eternity of dark winter.

But Jesus, the innocent one, makes the choice to die for Adam's sin, for all sin. He, like Aslan, rose from the dead, proving that He was God Himself. In so doing, He destroyed the power of the white witch, Satan himself, forever!

WHY NOT SOME OTHER WAY?

Why did Jesus have to die? Why couldn't God just snap His fingers and declare us holy? Why did blood have to be shed? The answer is simple: Jesus had to die for us to be able to go to heaven because God is a holy God and demands that every sin is fully punished. Jesus died on the cross because there was no other way for us to be saved. Someone had to die. Either we, the guilty, or He, the innocent. There are no in-betweens with God.

ASHLEY AND THE NONRELIGIOUS JESUS

Ashley had been a Jehovah's Witness as a child but rebelled against her family's belief system as a teenager. It was too narrow and constricting for a wild-hearted teenager filled with hopes and hormones. Although Ashley had been living a lifestyle the last few years that was out of line with her strict upbringing, she had been slowly coming to the realization that something was missing. Her time in God's Word and God's creation during the GOSPEL Journey adventure rekindled a desire in her heart to reconnect with God in a deeper, relational way.

When I began to explain the real, relevant, and nonreligious Jesus, I could see the glimmer of hope in her eyes. She was raised with the religious Jesus, the rule Jesus, the party-pooper Jesus. But now she was hearing about the God who loved her enough to be tortured, mocked, and murdered . . . for her.

This Jesus was a whole new ball game and Ashley knew it . . . maybe for the first time.

Blood had to be spilled. Hebrews 9:22 tells us that "without the shedding of blood there is no forgiveness." In the Old Testament, an innocent lamb had to be slaughtered in the place of a sinful Jew to satisfy God's righteous demands temporarily. In the new covenant Jesus Christ, the Lamb of God, was sacrificed in our stead to satisfy God's holy requirements eternally. As the perfect man, Jesus could die for sinful man. As eternal God, that death payment was infinite.

As difficult as it may be for us to comprehend, the epicenter of our faith is a slaughterhouse where only one lamb was killed . . . the Lamb of God. This historical event was propelled by God's love for us and God's hatred of sin. The significance of that brutal murder 2,000 years ago changed the world forever.

Jesus Christ, the Lion and the Lamb, sacrificed in our place for our sin!

And three days later, He rose from the dead, conquering death and sin once and for all!

Now that we are standing at the foot of the rope bridge, we realize it is drenched with the blood of Jesus Himself. It cost Him His life; He built it with His own hands and sanctified it with His own death. The rope bridge is the cross of Christ that spans the gap completely and repairs what Adam and Eve broke.

We stand in awe of how this little bridge could span such an awesome gap.

And now comes the tough part . . . putting our faith in it enough to take the first steps across so that we can complete our journey to the other side.

CHAPTER 13

EVERYONE WHO TRUSTS IN HIM HAS ETERNAL LIFE

The sun is breaking through the clouds, the last patches of fog are burning away and we can see the dazzling mountain sky on the other side of the rope bridge. The beautiful panorama across the chasm stands in stark contrast to the smell of rot and death in our nostrils and the weed-filled landscape that surrounds us. We can't wait to get to the other side. But it's going to take faith in something we've never stood on before. It's going to take stepping off the "safe" ground of our own human efforts and putting our trust in something that somebody else built.

◆ ◆ ◆

THE GOSPEL OF JOHN

The whole book of John was written to unbelievers who needed to understand that the strength of the "rope bridge" was enough to get them to the other side. The book demonstrates how Jesus did miracle after miracle, culminating with the miracle of His resurrection from the dead, to prove that He was who He claimed to be, the way to eternal life, the rope bridge that everyone can trust. John 20:31 explains why the book was written: "But these are written that you may believe that Jesus is the Christ, the Son of God, and that by believing you may have life in his name."

As a matter of fact, the book of John uses the word "believe" 98 times, mostly to describe the way to heaven! Jesus put it this way in John 6:47: "I tell you the truth, he who believes has everlasting life."

The word "believe" here doesn't mean that you just believe that Jesus existed. It actually means "to trust in, to rely upon completely." In other words, to receive the gift of eternal life you must trust in Jesus alone to forgive your sins. It takes more than just

BEN'S BEHAVIOR

Ben was one of the coolest Christians I have ever met. He wasn't forceful with his faith, but he wasn't shy about it either. He would wait for conversations to unfold, whether it was in the hot tub, on the rafting trip, or in the van, and then chime in with a penetrating comment or a great question. He spent so much time listening that when he talked, everybody listened. Sure, there were those who disagreed with Ben, but everyone respected him.

Ben's faith in Jesus was evident in his attitude, his actions, his sly smile, his listening ear, and his caring heart. Ben knew that there was only one way to heaven, through faith in Christ alone, but he never communicated this controversial message in an offensive way. Ben was grace in action, and his grace made a huge impact.

believing that He existed; it takes putting your full reliance upon Him to forgive you for all of your sins!

Once you believe in Him you become a child of God forever. John 1:12 tells us, "Yet to all who received him, to those who believed in his name, he gave the right to become children of God."

Not only that, but you are guaranteed eternal life in heaven. In John 5:24 Jesus said, "I tell you the truth, whoever hears my word and believes him who sent me has eternal life and will not be condemned; he has crossed over from death to life."

Eternal life is not a matter of trying but trusting. Trusting Jesus as your only hope of going to heaven is the most important decision of your life.

◆ ◆ ◆

What does all this mean for us on the GOSPEL Journey? Simply this: When we put our faith and trust in Christ alone for the forgiveness of sins, we enter into a personal, permanent relationship with God called eternal life. Moving from the slippery ledge of uncertainty we walk onto a bridge drenched red in the blood of Christ, a bridge that can never break, a bridge that will get us across the chasm of separation between sinful man and holy God, a bridge that is "the way and the truth and the life."

CHAPTER 14

LIFE THAT'S ETERNAL MEANS WE WILL BE WITH JESUS FOREVER

As we make our way across the bridge, we can't help but see the beautiful mountain crest on the other side. It represents our total salvation from sin, our escape from our previously cold, miserable existence when we were surrounded by fear and death. Through Christ's death we have been delivered from the penalty of sin, we are being delivered from the power of sin day after day, and we will be totally delivered from the presence of sin someday when we are with Jesus in heaven, at the highest point of the mountain.

We take our first steps onto this promised land of heavenly hope. The sunshine begins drying out our wet gear and its warmth penetrates deep inside us. But we're not in heaven yet. We have put our faith in Christ, taken the first step across the rope bridge of faith, and received the gift of eternal life. Now we are on a quest toward heaven. We have received eternal life and must walk the pathway of spiritual maturity, growing in our relationship with God every day.

◆ ◆ ◆

QUALITY OF LIFE

Contrary to popular opinion, eternal life doesn't start when you die. It starts as soon as you put your faith in Christ. Jesus put it this way: "Now this is eternal life: that they may know you, the only true God, and Jesus Christ, whom you have sent" (John 17:3).

Take note of what Jesus is saying. The essence of eternal life is a personal relationship with God. It is the quality of this life that Jesus focuses on, not the quantity of it. The beauty of being "saved" is not just what we are saved from, but what we are saved to. We are saved from hell. That's great. I don't want to go there. Neither do you. But we are saved to a beautiful relationship with our brand-new spiritual Daddy, who just happens to be the God of this universe.

Realize what this implies. Eternal life starts as soon as you believe. As soon as you are declared a child of God, you are baptized into relationship with your Creator—that is amazing. You have free access to the very throne room of the King of Kings, because now you are a prince or a princess. You can talk to Him any time of the day or night, no matter how far you have fallen, no matter where you are or who you are with. He is there, ready, willing, and able to answer you.

Not only can we talk to Him any time of the day or night, but He can talk to us as well. He has given us 66 love letters that express His mind on everything from relationships to finances to the character of God to the future of humanity. In the pages of Scripture we learn about Him, what He loves, and what He loathes. We discover how to please Him and how to serve Him.

Eternal life is a personal relationship with Jesus Christ that just happens to be permanent. It is a two-way street of fellowship and communion where He talks to us and we talk to Him.

QUANTITY OF LIFE

Eternal life is eternal. That's a given. That's why it's called eternal life. When we put our faith and trust in Jesus Christ we are entering a covenant relationship with the God of this universe that can never be broken by us and will never be broken by Him. The blood of Jesus Christ Himself sealed the deal forever.

Jude 24 ensures us that He is "able to keep you from falling and to present you before his glorious presence without fault and with great joy." Here are some verses that show us that eternal life lasts forever:

> "All that the Father gives me will come to me, and whoever comes to me I will never drive away. For I have come down from heaven not to do my will but to do the will of him who sent me. And this is the will of him who sent me, that I shall lose none of all that he has given me, but raise them up at the last day." (John 6:37-39)

◆

> "I give them eternal life, and they shall never perish; no one can snatch them out of my hand." (John 10:28)

◆

> For I am convinced that neither death nor life, neither angels nor demons, neither the present nor the future, nor any powers, neither height nor depth, nor anything else in all creation, will be able to separate us from the love of God that is in Christ Jesus our Lord. (Romans 8:38-39)

◆

Being confident of this, that he who began a good work in you will carry it on to completion until the day of Christ Jesus. (Philippians 1:6)

◆

Therefore he is able to save completely those who come to God through him, because he always lives to intercede for them. (Hebrews 7:25)

◆

God has said, "Never will I leave you; never will I forsake you." (Hebrews 13:5)

Think of it this way. When you were a child and you disobeyed your dad, did he throw you out of the house for good? Probably not. He brought you in and gave you a spanking, scolding, or time out. The same is true of our heavenly Father. When we sin He proves that He loves us through disciplining us. This heavenly "time out" could come in the form of a trial or a problem, a sickness or a struggle. He knows how to get our attention and teach us what He desires us to learn. When God spanks, it stings.

When sharing the good news with someone who doesn't know Jesus, it is vital to help that person understand that when one believes in Christ, he or she is entering into a wonderful relationship with Jesus Christ that is personal, permanent, and unshakeable. This assurance will give that new believer the confidence of a secure relationship that can propel him or her into a lifetime of thankful service to God. But this person needs to realize that once he or she has come to Christ, serving Him is not optional. Christ demands our all. If we don't give it, then He will discipline us until we do.

Once we traverse the rope bridge of Christ and plant our feet firmly on the other side, in one sense, our journey is over. We have crossed the gaping chasm and received the free gift of eternal life. We find ourselves in the midst of breathtaking beauty, gazing in awe at the splendor of our new surroundings. We have entered into an unbreakable, unshakeable relationship with Jesus. We have become a child of God.

In another sense our journey is just beginning. Once we take the last step off the rope bridge, the pathway continues toward the distant crest of the mountain called heaven. Our pack feels lighter, and we move forward with renewed energy. The pathway is our spiritual

---

TIFFANY'S VOICE

At the very end of the GOSPEL Journey, we all hugged and cried and shared. This was one wild week. Throughout the week I had been hearing how beautiful Tiffany's singing voice was. So I asked Tiffany if she would wrap up the week by singing a song. With the Rocky Mountains as her backdrop, she sang the most beautiful live rendition of "On My Knees" that I have ever heard.

What a beautiful end to our week in the mountains, to our GOSPEL Journey. In many ways Tiffany's song was a brief glimpse of the power and beauty of eternal life. When we put our faith in Christ we enter into a song, a beautiful ballad of hope. The song begins when we put our faith in Christ, and it never ends. Someday in heaven all our songs will harmonize as we surround the throne of Christ and get on our knees to worship our Creator, Redeemer, Lord, and Friend . . . forever.

growth in our newfound relationship with Jesus. Obstacles still creep onto our path, but we discover there are fellow travelers on this same path who are willing to walk alongside us and help us. We must get plugged into relationship with other Christians in a good local church and youth group. We must learn how to study the trail map of God's Word, pray, live in the power of the Spirit, and take others on the GOSPEL Journey.

CHAPTER 15

HOW TO TAKE YOUR FRIENDS ON THE GOSPEL JOURNEY

So now you understand the GOSPEL Journey. It's the ultimate love story. It's more than history, it's *His* story . . . and our story ties right in along the way.

So how do you take your friends on this exciting journey? How do you explain it to them in a way that they can understand?

While the gospel is a simple message, sometimes sharing it can be a tough undertaking. Many motivated Christian teens don't know what to say. Many informed Christian teens don't care to say it. Hopefully, by now you have the motivation. I just shared with you the information. It's time now to learn the application—how to share the gospel message in a clear and compelling way.

MEMORIZE THE GOSPEL ACRONYM WORD FOR WORD

I wish I had an easier way for you to do this. Memorization is not a popular thing. But if you are going to effectively communicate your faith, you must cut against the grain. You must do what it takes to master, not a method, but the gospel message.

The six points of the GOSPEL acronym are the key points in the gospel message:

God created us to be with Him.
Our sins separate us from God.
Sins cannot be removed by good deeds.
Paying the price for sin, Jesus died and rose again.
Everyone who trusts in Him alone has eternal life.
Life that's eternal means we will be with Him forever.

Why is it important to memorize these points word for word? They cover the span of the whole story of the Bible from Genesis chapter 1 to Revelation chapter 22. They cover every major point of the gospel message that a person should know, understand, and accept if he or she is going to become a Christian.

There's another reason you should memorize these six points. Mastering the GOSPEL will give you confidence as you communicate the message. It gives you key points to discuss along the pathway toward eternal life. It keeps you on track in the conversation.

As you know, when you are talking with a friend, the conversation can turn on a dime in another direction. Each of the points

How do you memorize something and seal it into your long-term memory? Write down what you are trying to memorize word for word, read it for a minute or two, then five minutes later read it again. In an hour do the same thing again, three hours later do it again, six hours later do it again, and do it one more time before you fall asleep. Repeat this three times a day for the second and third day. Studies show that if you've done that, you will have it sealed in your long-term memory. In other words, it will be hard to forget it. Want to make it easier? Try it with a friend or two or memorize it as a youth group this way. There is power in the tribe.

gives you ways to guide the discussion so that you can continue the journey toward Jesus.

USE THE GOSPEL JOURNEY AS A GUIDE, NOT A SCRIPT

If you just start quoting the GOSPEL Journey to someone, they may think you are crazy. This is a conversation guide, not a full script; you write the script in your own words. You will just make sure in the midst of this conversation that you are focusing on each point, one at a time, until you are finished.

Let me give you an example of how the conversation could go. See if you can find each point of the GOSPEL in this conversation. Let's say you are talking to your close friend Jake:

You: What are your spiritual beliefs, Jake?

Jake: I don't really know what I believe.

You: Well, if I could tell you how you could know that you were going to heaven, would that be good news?

Jake: I guess so.

You: You guess so? What do you mean by "you guess so"? This is important to me and it should be important to you, too! Do you want to just drift through life not knowing what you believe or whether or not you'll go to heaven when you die? So, do you want to know or not?

Jake: Calm down, freak. I want to know.

You: Okay, I'm better now. Sorry about that. I just—

Jake: Stop backpedaling and tell me what you've got to say. I want to know where you're headed with this.

You: Well, I'm going to tell you the whole story of Christianity, the whole message of it. I think a lot of times

it gets portrayed incorrectly by the media, and sometimes by Christians themselves.

Jake: Yeah, like some of those freaky TV preachers?

You: Exactly. But the real story of Christianity is an awesome story. It starts a long time ago when God created us to be with Him. He made Adam and Eve,
the first man and woman, put them in a garden,
and wanted to totally pour out His love on them.

Jake: You mean to tell me that you don't believe in evolution? I mean . . .

*The conversation continues about evolution and creation for a
few minutes.*

You: I'm sure that we could talk about this all day. But
to be honest, it's not the most crucial thing that
you need to understand about the story of Christianity. My point is that God created us to be with
Him. His original intent is to pour out His love on
all of humanity.

Jake: So God made us to love us, right?

You: Yes.

Jake: Then why is there so much pain and suffering in
the world?

You: That's a great question, Jake. As a matter of fact, it's
a perfect segue into the next part of the story of
Christianity. After God created Adam and Eve to be
in relationship with Him, they sinned. When they
sinned, they ensured the future of all humanity—
eternal separation from God. You see, our sins
separate us from God. As a result of the sin of

Adam and Eve, death, pain, and suffering entered the world.

Jake: So you're saying that all the suffering in the world is not God's fault? It's Adam and Eve's fault?

You: That's exactly what I'm saying. But it's our fault, too. We keep Adam and Eve's sinful legacy going every time we lie, lust, cheat, or steal. It's all of our faults. But it started with Adam and Eve. God put them both in a perfect environment, no sin, no problems, no pain. They chose to mess everything up. As a result, not only is this world condemned, but everybody in it is as well.

Jake: Are you talking about hell?

You: Yes.

Jake: That seems kind of harsh. God condemns everybody to hell because of Adam and Eve's sin.

You: And their own sin.

Jake: It still seems kind of brutal to me.

You: When you think about it, hell is the ultimate example of free will. God doesn't make everybody believe in Him. He gives them the choice to spend eternity with Him in heaven or eternal separation from Him in hell.

Jake: Well, who wants to go to hell? That's why people try to live a good life, right? To go to heaven and avoid hell.

You: But going to heaven is not by being good. As a matter of fact, sins could never be removed by our good deeds.

Jake: You mean to tell me that being good doesn't get you to heaven?

You: Not even close. The problem is that nobody could be good enough. God is a perfect God and demands perfection of all who dwell in heaven. The Bible makes it clear in Revelation 21:27 that even if you just told one little white lie you could never make it into heaven. To get into heaven we have to be as good as God Himself.

Jake: That seems a little unrealistic, doesn't it?

You: Yes. It is totally unrealistic. It can't be done.

Jake: So is there any good news here in this story of Christianity? Right now it all seems pretty bad to me.

You: Yeah, here is where it starts getting good, really good. After thousands of years of people trying to earn their way to heaven by good deeds, God sent His own Son to become the God-man and live the perfect life that we could never live. Then paying the price for sin, Jesus died and rose again.

Jake: So you're saying that Jesus Christ died for my sins? Why in the world would God die in my place?"

You: Jesus gave the answer in John 3:16: "For God so loved the world that he gave his one and only Son, that whoever believes in him shall not perish but have eternal life." The answer is because God loves you enough to sacrifice His own Son for your sins.

Jake: So there's nothing I have to do to get to heaven? If Jesus died for everybody's sin then everybody's going to heaven?

You: No. Everybody's not going to heaven. To have your sins forgiven you must receive what He did for you.

Jake: What does that mean, "receive"?

You: It means you put your faith in Jesus to forgive you for your sins based on what He did for you on the cross. Everyone who trusts in Him alone has eternal life.

Jake: Trusts in Him alone?

You: Yes! He said in John 14:6 that He is "the way, the truth, and the life." He said that nobody comes to the heavenly Father except through Him.

Jake: That sounds kind of exclusive and narrow-minded.

You: It is, Jake! Maybe that's why Jesus said that broad is the road that leads to destruction and narrow is the path that leads to eternal life. That narrow path is faith in Jesus alone for salvation. But if you think about it, if Jesus is God and if He loved us enough to die for us on the cross, then He can set the rules of engagement.

Jake: I guess that's the key point—"if Jesus is God." I'm not so sure He is. I think Jesus was a good man.

You: A good man who claimed to be God? Come on, Jake. If He is not God then He is either a liar or a kook. And if He is a kook then I'm one, too, for following Him. But if He is God, then He is the way, the only way to eternal life.

Jake: Okay, so let's say I trust in Him. What next?

You: Realize that you receive the free gift of eternal life, and life that's eternal means you will be with Jesus forever . . . starting now.

> Jake: I don't know. That's just a lot of stuff to think about. I don't know if I'm ready yet.
>
> You: Well, I'm not going to force you into a relationship with God, but I want to continue this conversation. In a lot of ways it's the most important issue of life.
>
> Jake: You're right. Let's talk again about this. I appreciate your willingness to bring it up with me. Even though, my friend, you are a kook.
>
> *Both laugh.*

THE JOURNEY HAS BEGUN

This "script" is an example of how you can use the GOSPEL Journey as talking points in the natural ebb and flow of conversation with your friends. Obviously, no two conversations are exactly the same. But this sample will give you an idea of the way a good two-way dialogue between you and a friend could unfold. If you look closely at the dialogue you can see that every point of the GOSPEL was referred to throughout the conversation. Jake never knew that an acrostic was being covered in their talk. It was memorized and used as a guide, not a script.

Add in Other Illustrations to Help Make Your Point

You can use illustrations in a powerful way to make your point. These illustrations can range from personal ones (like the time you took a leap of faith from a rock cliff into the water below or something else to illustrate faith) to stand-alone illustrations (like the ones I'm about to share with you). The point is that a picture paints a thousand words. I've developed most of the following illustrations after thousands of experiences sharing the gospel over the last 30 years or so of my life. You can choose what fits you best or use your own illustrations to help make the point. I'm going to give you illustrations that you can use each step of the GOSPEL Journey.

God created us to be with Him
◆ *The Ant Pile*

Did you ever know a little kid who loved to take a magnifying glass, put it up to the sky, and use the intensified rays to burn ants in an ant pile (or were you that kid)? Sometimes kids can be cruel. They may laugh but the ants don't think it's funny. Some people view God the same way. They think that He loves to use His magnifying glass to burn people with catastrophes and problems. Nothing could be further from the truth. As a matter of fact, God created us to be with Him. He made the first man and woman to be in perfect relationship with Him in the perfect environment, to pour out His love on them.

Our sins separate us from God
◆ *Throwing Rocks at the Moon*

You could try throwing a rock and hitting the moon, but you'll never come close. You may throw it farther than me, or anybody on this earth for that matter, but you wouldn't have a chance. The moon is more than 238,000 miles away from the earth. Even if you could throw a rock one mile high you wouldn't even start coming close to having what it takes to hit the moon with a rock.

The same is true with getting into heaven. God's standard for getting into heaven is perfection. We're not even close. You could be the nicest person on the planet and you wouldn't stand a chance of being as good as God. We all miss the mark of God's perfection. By the way, that's what the word "sin" means—"to miss the mark." Our sins separate us from God.

◆ Swimming the Ocean

Imagine that you and I are standing on the coast of California and we decide to swim to Hawaii. Maybe you make it 15 miles and I make it five or so. It doesn't matter. Because both of us are going to end up dead in the water. Why? It is too far for anyone to swim. It is not humanly possible. In the same way, if we try to make it to heaven by living a good life then we are going to fall way short. Why? According to the Bible we have to be as good as God to get into heaven. Nobody is. So we all miss the mark of God's impossible standard.

Sins cannot be removed by good deeds
◆ White Frosting/Burned Cake

Let's say that I baked you a cake and burned it badly. If I were to cover it in white frosting and give it to you, the cake would still be burned even though you couldn't see it. As soon as you bit into it you would know. Putting white frosting on a burned cake doesn't change the fact that the cake is ruined. Covering our sinful lives with good deeds doesn't change the fact that we have sinned. God sees right through the "frosting" straight to our sin.

Paying the price for sin, Jesus died and rose again
◆ The Truck

Imagine walking across a busy intersection during rush hour. Suddenly, a speeding truck comes out of nowhere and is heading directly at you. You are not paying close attention and don't see the truck. But someone standing on the corner does. He runs into the street and pushes you out of the way. That person absorbs the full impact of the truck and is killed instantly. This hero took your place in death. He sacrificed his life for yours. In the same way God's anger for sin was headed full speed at you. Christ pushed you out of the way and sacrificed His life so that you could live forever. He died in your place and mine!

Everyone who trusts in Him alone has eternal life
◆ *The Chair*
If you trust in a chair then you are willing to sit on it, to put your full weight upon it. If you say that you believe the chair could hold your weight but you're not willing to put your full weight upon it, then you don't have real faith. When it comes to Jesus, it takes more than just believing that Jesus can forgive you for all your sins; it takes putting your full weight upon Him in faith.

Life that's eternal means we will be with Jesus forever
◆ *The River*
Eternal life is like a river that goes on forever. But this river is just as deep as it is long. You can never reach the end of the river or the bottom of it. It is eternal in both directions. You see, eternal life is more than just living forever, more than an eternal quantity of time. It's deep, an infinite quality of life, a life that will continue forever in an ever-deepening relationship with the God of the universe.

Don't give up on your friends if they don't want to listen to you talk about the GOSPEL. Keep praying for them. Remember that somebody didn't give up on you.

CHAPTER 16

HOW TO BRING YOUR FRIENDS TO A POINT OF DECIDING

Okay, you've shared the gospel with your friend. What do you do now? You ask him or her two simple questions:

> 1. Did that make sense? (If it didn't, go over it again, maybe using some more of the illustrations you learned in the last chapter. If it did make sense, then move on to the next question.)
> 2. Would you trust in Jesus as your only hope of eternal life with God?

While bringing up the gospel with your friends may be the most uncomfortable part of sharing the gospel, this last question is a close second. Why? It puts them on the spot. It causes them to verbalize whether or not they will accept or reject Jesus as the one who will save them from their sins.

Why is this important? Because, quite honestly, if they don't trust in Christ today and they die tomorrow, then they will be separated from God in hell forever. Maybe that's why the apostle Peter pushed his listeners so hard to come to Christ right away in Acts 2:40: "With many other words he warned them; and he pleaded with them, 'Save yourselves from this corrupt generation.'"

Maybe that's why God reminds us in 2 Corinthians 6:2, "I tell you, now is the time of God's favor, now is the day of salvation." There's no better time than today to trust in Christ as your only hope of forgiveness, because there's no guarantee of tomorrow.

Remember Jesus' parable of the sower as you share your faith! Here are the words of Jesus in Mark 4:3-9:

> "Listen! A farmer went out to sow his seed. As he was scattering the seed, some fell along the path, and the birds came and ate it up. Some fell on rocky places, where it did not have much soil. It sprang up quickly, because the soil was shallow. But when the sun came up, the plants were scorched, and they withered because they had no root. Other seed fell among thorns, which grew up and choked the plants, so that they did not bear grain. Still other seed fell on good soil. It came up, grew and produced a crop, multiplying thirty, sixty, or even a hundred times."
>
> Then Jesus said, "He who has ears to hear, let him hear."

Jesus is reminding His disciples here that not all of those they share the message with will respond with a "Yes, I believe!" He goes on to explain that some who hear the message will have the message scavenged by Satan. Others will seem to accept it but will have no spiritual roots and fizzle out or be choked by the weeds of worldliness. But some seeds they sow will fall on fertile ground and multiply. Don't get discouraged if not everybody responds positively to the gospel message! Go with the growers and pray for the others! Keep sharing and keep asking them to respond.

FISHING WITHOUT REELING

I was raised in a fisherman's home. My grandpa was a fisherman. He took me fishing a lot when I was a kid. He taught me how to bait the hook, cast the line, wait for the bite, set the hook into the fish's jaw with a flick of the wrist, and then reel it in. I can't imagine him telling me to go through all of the hassle of hooking the fish without reeling it in after it bites.

Although fishing is kind of a crude analogy to sharing one's faith (but don't be mad at me . . . Jesus started it!), I think the point is strong. When we bait the hook by sparking people's interest in spiritual things, and then set the hook by sharing the gospel

---

WARNING!

As you share the gospel, remember that for some people coming to Christ will be a short trip, and for others it will be a long journey. Some of your friends may respond right away to the gospel. Others may take a while to come around. Never give up! It took 12 years of praying and a case of life-threatening cancer to finally convince my Uncle Richard to trust in Christ as his Savior. I started sharing the gospel with him when I was 15 years old. He finally came to Christ when I was 27. Within a few months, he was in heaven. It was worth every conversation, every prayer, every sleepless night. I can't wait to see him someday. Don't give up on your friends who are on the longer journey to Jesus!

with them, it only makes sense to reel them into the family of God by asking them the right questions after they hear the message.

After you take your friends on the GOSPEL Journey, help them to complete the trip by asking them the two key questions.

Today is the day of salvation!

CHAPTER 17

HOW TO KEEP THE MESSAGE CLEAR TO YOUR FRIENDS

I don't know what it is with Christians. They love to use terms that confuse the simplicity of the gospel. Even questions like "Are you a Christian?" can be confusing because most people in America think of themselves as Christians in one sense or another. But being born in America doesn't make you a Christian, just as being born in a garage doesn't make you a car.

It is vital as we share the gospel with our friends, teammates, classmates, family members, and neighbors that we are as clear as possible. Here are a few terms to avoid.

1. Are You Saved?

Saved from what? Saved from boredom or from a fire in the building? Saved from a school bully or a bad teacher?

Replace this term with words everyone can understand, like "Do you know you are going to heaven?" or "Are you sure God has forgiven you for all your sins?"

2. Let Jesus into Your Heart.

I'll never forget my Sunday-school teacher challenging us every week during class (after the flannel-graph special-effects show) to "let Jesus into our hearts."

Being the neurotic little kid that I was, I had this mental picture of Jesus desperately trying to squeeze into each ventricle of my heart. Somehow I was unknowingly blocking Him from coming into my heart with some subconscious brain impulse that was impeding my salvation.

But part of my perplexity was my Sunday-school teacher's fault. Although she was doing her best to give the gospel, she was unintentionally confusing me with a term that has been sacredly handed down from generation to generation of traditional American Christians.

3. Turn from All Your Sin.

Okay, this is a biggie. I mean, we all want sinners to turn from their sins right? We want them to live a life that pleases God and to rid themselves of their naughty, sinful habits. The problem is, if we are honest, we are still sinners ourselves. When we tell them that they must "turn from their sin" to receive the gift of eternal life, we are asking non-Christians to do something that we are still struggling with ourselves. We are asking them to do something that is an ongoing result of salvation, not a prerequisite to salvation.

Instead we ought to make sure they trust in Christ as their only hope for the forgiveness of their sins first. Once they trust in Christ, their sins are forgiven. They are given the power and desire to turn from their sins. They enter that lifelong struggle of turning from their sins and only fully succeed when they die.

Even the super apostle Paul struggled right up to the end to turn from his sin. Listen to his words to the early Christians:

> For I have the desire to do what is good, but I cannot carry it out. For what I do is not the good I want to do;

no, the evil I do not want to do—this I keep on doing.
Now if I do what I do not want to do, it is no longer I
who do it, but it is sin living in me that does it. (Romans
7:18-20)

If Paul still struggled with turning from his sin and living a
life that pleased God, how can we ask an unbeliever who has no
internal capacity to choose what is truly good to do what we cannot? Let's get them to trust in Christ first so that the Holy Spirit
can come into their lives and begin the never-ending process of
turning them from their sin!

4. Just Say this Prayer . . .

I cringe when I hear Christians use this term with teenagers as a
requirement for salvation. Saying "the sinner's prayer" has almost
become a magic potion of sorts for some believers. It's almost as
though they think that if they can just get somebody to say it,
then he or she is saved from sin, death, and hell.

But merely saying a prayer never saved anyone. Jesus never
led anybody through the sinner's prayer, and neither did Paul,
Peter, nor any of the other apostles. Why? Because there are no
magic words that will bring somebody into the family of God.
Faith in Christ alone is the only way.

Saying a prayer after the moment of salvation is a great way
for the new believer to thank God for the free gift of salvation. But
making it a requirement for salvation is a bad idea. I am convinced
that there will be many people in hell who said the sinner's prayer.
Why? Because it's easier to just say the words than it is to actually
put your faith and trust in a person you've never met to take you
somewhere you have never been.

PUT YOURSELF IN THEIR SHOES

As you share your faith, always try to remember to put yourself in their shoes. Understanding their point of reference will help you clearly share the gospel message. In other words, some of your friends who have no religious or spiritual background whatsoever may not understand what basic terms like "salvation" or "savior" mean. Maybe instead of "salvation" use the phrase "forgiveness and cleansing from the things we've done wrong." Instead of "savior" use "the one who saves us from our sin." Just be careful and be aware. If you do use a word or term that you sense they don't understand, simply explain what that word or phrase means.

If you aren't sure that your friends understand, ask them if what you are saying makes sense. Take a little extra time to present to them a clear message. When in doubt, spell it out!

CHAPTER 18

HOW TO SHARE YOUR OWN STORY

When you share the gospel message, it is important to be able to articulate your own story, the story of your personal journey to Jesus. Some people call this a "personal testimony." In a court case, somebody who provides testimony shares what he or she has seen and heard, and what has happened to him or her. In this case, you are sharing what you saw and heard that changed your mind about Christ, and what has happened to you since.

A credible testimony in a court case is hard to deny. It's hard to deny when you're sharing your faith as well. People may be able to argue the facts night and day with you, but it is difficult to deny somebody's personal experience.

The apostle Paul shared his personal story of coming to Jesus in Acts 26 before King Agrippa. It was difficult for this king to deny the authenticity of Paul's story. As a matter of fact, he didn't even try.

The same is true of you and your friends. As you share your story with them, it will be tough for them to say "That's not true!" because you are sharing what you know to be the truth from your own experience.

The challenge is understanding how to share your story in a compelling and authentic way.

SHARING A COMPELLING PERSONAL STORY

A good personal story describing how you came to put your faith in Jesus has three components:

1. A Before-and-After Factor

Have you ever seen one of those TV weight-loss commercials? Almost all of them have one thing in common—the Before-and-After Factor. Those television testimonials usually go something like this:

> Here is how I looked before I took Fat-B-Gone [picture of overweight guy without a shirt] and here is how I look now [picture of same guy this time about 100 pounds lighter with firm muscles and tanned skin]. If you use Fat-B-Gone you could be just like me! For only a small investment of $1,000 per bottle your life could be transformed forever. Thanks, Fat-B-Gone!

Can you imagine somebody trying to sell a weight-loss product where the person actually got fatter after taking it? Ridiculous! The whole point of "selling" is making a case for how your life is better after product X than it was before it. Whether it be weight loss, whiter teeth, better gas mileage, or faster downloads, selling something to someone else requires that a person be convinced that his or her life will be better after using product X than it was before.

Well, the gospel is not a product, and sharing your faith is not selling—how can you sell something that's free to begin with?—but the same principle applies. There should be a difference in your life after you have experienced Jesus. If not, then why "buy"?

Maybe your personal story goes something like this:

Before I trusted in Christ I was partying a lot. I came to realize that this was a dead end. To be honest, I got sick of the morning-after guilt. That's when my friend shared Jesus with me and I became a Christian. Since then I haven't been perfect. There have been times I've struggled with my old way of life. But for the most part, I've been seeking to serve Jesus and the morning-after guilt is gone. I have a new reason to party . . . but it's a whole different kind of party.

Or maybe it's more like this:

I became a Christian when I was a little kid. I don't remember much before then except for the fear that I had in my mind of dying. I think I saw some movie that talked about hell or something and ever since then I was afraid of what was going to happen to me after I died. One day in Sunday school my teacher, Mrs. Johnson, was talking about how we could know for sure we were going to heaven someday. I was ready to hear it. That day I trusted in Jesus, and ever since then I have had the assurance of knowing I was going to heaven someday.

However your story unfolds, there needs to be a Before-and-After Factor. You need to share how your life has been different since, whether it be stopping the party life or getting assurance of going to heaven someday.

2. The Turning Point

The second key to an effective personal story is sharing the turning point. What was it that helped convince you to believe in Jesus as your only hope for eternal life? Was it the lifestyle of a friend who had something you didn't? Was it a camp message where you realized all that Jesus had endured for you? Was it the feeling of guilt in your heart after doing something you knew you shouldn't have? Was it the fear of death or hell?

Whatever that turning point situation, feeling, or thought was, just realize that it was sent from God to help turn you toward Him.

3. An Authentic Honesty

Nobody's perfect. Have you ever met somebody who thinks he is? Mr. or Miss Perfect tends to make all of us a little nauseated. People don't like to be around plastic people unless they themselves are plastic too.

When it comes to sharing Jesus, don't try to come off as perfect or plastic. Share the story, your story, with grit and raw honesty.

Sure, there should be the primary difference that Jesus made in your life, the Before-and-After Factor, if you will. But you should be willing to share how you've struggled since meeting Jesus, too. As a matter of fact, when you think about it, the only difference between you and your unreached friends is that your sins are forgiven and theirs are not. That's why I love the old quote that describes sharing your faith as one beggar showing another beggar where to find bread. Every human on this planet is a spiritual beggar, longing for something to fill their appetite. The difference between Christians and the rest of the world is that we know the location of the pantry that holds the bread of life.

TIME TO TESTIFY!

Use the space below to write out an account of your personal journey to Jesus. Be sure to include the Before-and-After Factor—what changed in your life since meeting Jesus? Also include the turning point—what was the key person, feeling, or circumstance that led up to your conversion to Jesus? Be sure to be authentic as you share how your life has been since!

Before Factor
Describe how your life was before you met Jesus.

The Turning Point
Describe what led to you becoming a Christian.

After Factor
Describe how your life's been since. . . . Be authentic!

A TWO-MINUTE PERSONAL STORY

Now that you have written out your story word for word, it's time to memorize it and be able to share it in two minutes or less. Why? Because you never know when it will come in handy! Let's say that you are at a break between classes and you get into a conversation with one of your friends on the way to the next class. Your personal story is a great way to open the door to taking somebody else on the GOSPEL Journey.

Or let's say that you are sharing the gospel with a friend but he or she seems skeptical. That's where you can start sharing your personal story. Again, it's hard to deny somebody's own experience, especially the experience of a close friend.

Okay, now you've learned to talk. You've learned how to take somebody on the GOSPEL Journey. You've discovered how to share your own story. Now it's time to master one of the most difficult parts of sharing your faith—learning to listen, discovering how to have a two-way dialogue about spiritual truth.

CHAPTER 19

HOW TO HAVE
L³ CONVERSATIONS

I was never very good at formulas in geometry or trigonometry in high school. Perhaps it was because I could never figure out what good they would ever do me in real life. Since I didn't plan on becoming an engineer, a NASA scientist, or a math teacher, math formulas seemed kind of goofy to me.

But I studied and aced the classes anyway. Although formulas weren't my main concern in life, I knew I should do everything (yes, even math problems) for the glory of God. And I'm glad that I did. Many times a theorem came in handy when I worked a roofing construction job. What do you know? My math teacher was right. That stuff did matter . . . and guess what? The formulas worked!

So, are there any spiritual theorems for sharing Jesus with our friends? Believe it or not, yes! I have discovered one timeless axiom during 30 years of faith sharing with thousands of others (If you can't do the math, let me sum it up this way . . . I'm old!) that has helped me become immensely more effective. It's this:

$$\text{Loving}^3 \times \text{Listening}^3 \times \text{Learning}^3 = \text{Reaching}^3$$

I call this theorem L^3 for short.

Let me give you a basic explanation of this powerful faith-sharing formula. When you truly love people to the 3rd power, deeply listen to them in the 3rd power, and then learn from them and from God's Word in the 3rd power, then you can reach them on the deepest level with the message of God's Word.

This spiritual principle is tried-and-true because it is rooted in the pages of God's Word. Its truth is reaffirmed again and again in modern studies of the social dynamics of human interaction and communication. When you love somebody, listen to them, and learn from them and from God's Word, something powerful takes place—the unleashing of the gospel into the mind and soul of the person you are talking to. And when all of this is done in the 3rd power, the power of the third member of the Trinity—namely the Holy Spirit Himself—an unstoppable chain of events can lead to the person's eternal salvation!

Let's take a quick look at each of the components of L^3.

LOVING³

Loving to the 3rd power means caring deeply for those with whom we share the gospel. Your friends, classmates, teammates, neighbors, family members, and coworkers are not projects; they are people—people who desperately need the hope of Jesus. Our hearts need to be broken for them.

When we are controlled by the Holy Spirit, the first fruit He produces through us is love, according to Galatians 5:22. So if you are not loving the person as you share Jesus, you are not operating in the 3rd power, but instead in your own strength. And guess what? You are not strong enough to save a soul on your own.

We must love everyone we encounter with the affection of God Himself. Our hearts should be broken over their current spiritual condition and their future eternal destination. We should care about them, their lives, their hurts, and their questions.

One of the greatest evangelists who ever lived put it this way:

> If I speak in the tongues of men and of angels, but have not love, I am only a resounding gong or a clanging cymbal. If I have the gift of prophecy and can fathom all mysteries and all knowledge, and if I have a faith that can move mountains, but have not love, I am nothing. If I give all I possess to the poor and surrender my body to the flames, but have not love, I gain nothing. (1 Corinthians 13:1-3)

Without love we gain nothing, we do nothing, we are nothing. Love is the ultimate description of Christianity and should be our defining characteristic as representatives of the Lord Jesus.

Some famous verses in the 1 Corinthians 13 "love" passage describe how we should lovingly share Jesus with others:

> Love is patient, love is kind. It does not envy, it does not boast, it is not proud. It is not rude, it is not self-seeking, it is not easily angered, it keeps no record of wrongs. Love does not delight in evil but rejoices with the truth. It always protects, always trusts, always hopes, always perseveres. Love never fails. (verses 4-8)

Think about what this means for you as you share Jesus with those God brings across your path. We never have a right to be rude, impatient, angry, or arrogant. Instead we should be selfless, trusting, hopeful, positive, and persistent.

This kind of love is hard to resist.

So before you begin to share Jesus with those around you, take a look at the inside of your heart. Make sure that the stuff propelling you to share Jesus is love (the ultimate passion fuel) and not some other lesser thing.

LISTENING[3]

Listening to the 3rd power means depending on the Spirit of God to give us the wisdom to keep our mouths shut and our ears open as we encounter other belief systems. It means getting better at asking questions that create open, honest discussion. This works because teens (and most adults for that matter) usually love talking about themselves. They enjoy sharing their views on life, politics, school, work, and, yes, even their religion and spiritual beliefs.

Jesus was especially effective at asking people the right questions and then listening to their responses.

- In Matthew 16:15, Jesus asked Peter, "Who do you say that I am?"
- In Mark 10:18, Jesus asked the rich young ruler, "Why do you call me good?"
- In Luke 20:41-44, Jesus asked the religious leaders of his day why they believed what they believed about who the Christ or Messiah would be.

The list of questions Jesus asked goes on and on. He asked the people He encountered thought-provoking questions that triggered open and honest dialogue.

Asking good questions is all part of the discussion process.

Some questions you ask are for the purpose of learning more about what the other person believes. Other questions are asked with the intent of causing someone else to think.

Earlier in chapter 6 you learned some questions that could help get the conversation started. Here are some open-ended questions that can help keep the dialogue going in an open and honest way:

- How did your parents' spiritual beliefs influence you? Do you believe what they do or do you have a different perspective?
- Have you ever been to a church? How did you feel about your experience there? How did it impact or alter your view of Christians?
- Why do you think you hold the views of God that you do now? How have your views changed over the years?
- What do you think about Jesus? Do you think He was the Son of God, a good teacher, or something else?
- Why do you think there is so much suffering in the world? Why do you think God would allow it? Do you think God cares about humanity? About you?
- What are your views of the Bible? Have you read it? Do you think it is the Word of God or just some book put together by a bunch of men a long time ago? Why?

The list of possible questions is endless. The point is to ask questions that create open and honest discussion. And remember, the L³ theorem only works if you listen in love.

One of the ways we love others is by valuing them enough to listen to their point of view, even if it is dead wrong. But something almost miraculous happens when you listen so that you understand where somebody is coming from: That person will listen to understand where you are coming from as well. As you seek to deeply listen to others, they will be much more open to listening to you in return.

Never Argue as You Listen!

Most Mormon missionaries I've met refuse to argue. They don't mind discussing or disagreeing. They just want to make sure the conversation never gets heated or mean-spirited. While I absolutely disagree with my Mormon friends on many issues, I have learned from them how to argue without being argumentative.

Actually, if I had read and applied God's Word, I wouldn't have had to learn from the Mormons. The Bible tells us in 2 Timothy 2:23-26 how we should handle disagreements.

> Don't have anything to do with foolish and stupid arguments, because you know they produce quarrels. And the Lord's servant must not quarrel; instead, he must be kind to everyone, able to teach, not resentful. Those who oppose him he must gently instruct, in the hope that God will grant them repentance leading them to a knowledge of the truth, and that they will come to their senses and escape from the trap of the devil, who has taken them captive to do his will.

This passage isn't saying that we should always agree with everybody. It means very simply, that when we do disagree, we teach God's Word to them with kindness, gentleness, and patience instead of angry arguments.

There's an old saying that goes, "You can catch more flies with honey than with vinegar." What's true of flies is true of people too. You can convince more minds of the truth through love than hate, through gentleness than harshness, and through patient discussion than intense debate.

As I seek to apply this principle in my quest to share Jesus with others, I'm seeing much more effectiveness. If you apply this principle, you will too.

LEARNING³

As you love and listen to people, you learn in the process. You learn what they believe about life, God, heaven, hell, sin, and salvation. You learn where they are coming from, and once they feel like you are truly listening and learning from them, they are much more open to listen and learn from you.

So let's say you are talking to a girl at school who is a Buddhist. You find out all about where she is coming from. You aren't listening to argue, you are listening to learn, to truly understand

CAN I GET A WITNESS?

I'm Elizabeth. I'm 16 and from Colorado. I've talked to most of my friends about God. It's amazing because most of my friends are actually interested in talking about spiritual things. They aren't interested in the "I'm right, you're wrong" approach but they are interested in thinking and talking about the meaning of life and philosophical ideas. My friends are more receptive when I engage them in a discussion instead of us trying to prove each other wrong. When I ask my friends questions, they genuinely think about their views and question them instead of just dismissing God.

why she believes what she believes. The more you listen, the more she opens up. The more she shares. The more she trusts. And the more likely she is to listen to you when you start sharing Jesus.

After one or two really good conversations with your Buddhist friend, you feel as if you have a pretty good handle on what she believes and why she believes it. But the learning is not over. As a matter of fact it has just begun. Now you go back to your Bible, maybe do a little research online at www.dare2share.org, and talk to your parents and youth pastor to learn what the Bible says about these subjects.

When you continue the dialogue with your Buddhist friend, you are able to talk intelligently about what the Bible has to say about these various issues. You agree with her where you can agree and then lovingly share the truth from God's Word where you can't agree. But the learning doesn't stop there, because more likely than not, your Buddhist friend is going to bring up some really good points you have never considered. What do you do? You show her love by going back to the Bible (and your spiritual mentors) to learn even more. The dialogue continues.

Do you see what we are looking for? Not argument! This is not debate club. What we are looking for is real conversation, a two-way dialogue where both parties are listening and learning from each other and from the Bible.

In the process you learn what you believe, why you believe it, and where you can find it in the Bible. You also learn about your Buddhist friend's beliefs and background. And, believe me, the old adage is true, "You'll never argue somebody into the kingdom of God." But the Word of God, the Spirit of God, and the gospel of Christ will do their work in others' hearts as you share with a loving heart and two listening ears.

THE 3RD POWER

The most important part in Loving³, Listening³, and Learning³ is the 3rd power! If we do what we do in His strength and not our own, He will give us the wisdom we need to love, listen, and learn in this whole process of sharing Jesus with others. Check out this passage that reminds us of the importance of depending on the Spirit as we share Jesus:

> But when they arrest you, do not worry about what to say or how to say it. At that time you will be given what to say, for it will not be you speaking, but the Spirit of your Father speaking through you. (Matthew 10:19-20)

As you trust in the Spirit of God, He will spring forth love in your heart, the ability to listen, and the desire to learn. He will guide you in what to say as you share with your friends the greatest message on planet Earth. Depend on Him!

When you engage in genuine interactive sharing by loving people, listening to them, and learning from them, you begin to have deep and powerful communication. In this dialogue the gospel message is unleashed and begins to reach them at the deepest level. You get past petty excuses and little arguments and get to the core of their souls. In the process you come to appreciate them personally and respect how they have come to their beliefs.

Mastering this formula can revolutionize the way you share your faith. It will take time and effort, and at times you will probably fail. But don't be discouraged; after almost three decades of sharing Jesus, I'm still learning.

CHAPTER 20

HOW TO DEFEND YOUR FAITH WITHOUT BEING OFFENSIVE

So you've learned how to have an L³ conversation. Now it's time to learn how to defend your faith without being offensive to others.

Understanding that loving, listening, learning, and having a real dialogue is vitally important, we must be ready to challenge others to think. Once again it is important to re-emphasize here that I'm not talking about arguing. I'm talking about disagreeing with somebody in a kind, gentle, and thought-provoking way. All the "rules" of listening, loving, and learning in the last chapter still apply.

THE 4-1 DEFENSIVE FORMATION

This powerful tool for defending your faith is built around four key questions and one powerful statement. The questions are designed to get your friend to think, and the statement is designed to buy you some time. The questions were designed and/or compiled by my good friends Bill Jack, who is with The Worldview Academy in New Braunfels, Texas, and Andrew Heister.

The 4 Questions:
1. What do you mean by that?
2. How do you know that to be true?
3. What difference has it made in your life?
4. What if you're wrong?

Let's take a look at each of these questions and how you can use them as you defend your faith.

1. What do you mean by that? "What do you mean by that?" is a question designed to clarify. For instance, if you are sharing Jesus with your friends and they say that they are already Christians, you can ask the question, "What do you mean by 'Christian'?" Maybe they think that going to church automatically makes a person a Christian. Maybe they have actually put their faith in Christ already. But you don't know unless you clarify with this question.

Or let's say you are talking to a friend at school and he or she claims to be an agnostic. Ask your friend what he or she means by the word "agnostic." Again, this helps to clarify where your friend is coming from as you are sharing Jesus.

2. How do you know that to be true? While the first question clarifies, the second question, "How do you know that to be true?" explains. It explains your friends' line of thinking and reasoning for believing what they do. To be honest, this may cause your friends to ask themselves how they actually do know what they believe to be true.

3. What difference has it made in your life? When you ask the question "What difference has it made in your life?" you are getting a little personal and you are asking them to get the same. This question is especially handy with those philosophies that take God out of the equation altogether. If there is no God, no afterlife, what hope does a person have later and what assurance do they have now?

Those religions that have a works-based approach to achieving salvation are not much better when it comes to hope. A person trying to earn salvation can't walk in the confidence of an irrevocable, unshakeable love relationship with the God of the universe like a Christian can. Just getting someone to think this through can crack the door open in their mind for a belief system—like basic Christianity—that is more powerful in this life and offers total assurance for the next.

4. What if you're wrong? Out of all the four questions in the 4-1 Defensive Formation, "What if you're wrong?" is probably the most thought provoking. It forces a person to consider the eternal implications of being wrong about who Jesus is and how eternal life is obtained. I've seen this question work powerfully over the years. But the most impact I've ever seen it have was on an airplane trip to Johnson City, Tennessee, with a lady named Catherine.

You see, I work with an organization called Dare 2 Share Ministries. I travel with a large team of actors, musicians, and trainers from city to city training tens of thousands of teenagers every year to know, live, share, and own their faith.

> ## WARNING!
>
> It's at this point your friends may get a little defensive, especially if they can't come up with a good reason for how they know something to be true. Treat them with gentleness and respect. You don't want to win the argument and lose their soul. Your goal is to get them to think seriously and objectively about their own beliefs.

It was during this kind of trip, on a cramped commuter flight between Chicago and Johnson City, that I met Catherine.

She asked me why this big group of quasi-rowdy conference team members were all headed to Tennessee. I told her a little about what Dare 2 Share was all about. As soon as I mentioned the word "Christian" training conference, she begin to hammer me with question after question. Questions like:

- Do you believe that Jesus is the only way to heaven?
- What about the Jews, Hindus, and Muslims?
- What happens to those who reject Jesus?

These were just a few of the questions that Catherine asked me. To be honest, I wasn't much in the mood. I had a lot of computer work to do and was busy jamming away on my laptop. But God's Spirit had obviously opened a door of opportunity. So I took it.

I responded with the classic apologetic arguments from one of the great Christian thinkers of the twentieth century, C. S. Lewis. I explained to her that Jesus is either Lord, lunatic, or liar because He claimed again and again to be God in the flesh. From the hundreds of prophesies about Jesus that were completely fulfilled, to the weight of eyewitness testimony, I stacked the evidence of Christ's deity before her. She didn't blink.

"I believe that as long as you are sincere you will be okay," she retorted.

"What about Hitler? He was sincere," I shot back.

Again, she was cemented firmly in her convictions that my conclusions were too "narrow-minded." After several minutes of loaded discussion, I realized that I was getting nowhere. Although we were talking about some pretty intense subjects, neither of us raised our voice. This was an L^3 conversation (explained in chapter 19) and didn't have a hint of mean-spiritedness.

So I decided to break out the 4-1 Defensive Formation, specifically the last question.

"Catherine, let me ask you one thing. What if you are wrong?" I asked as the plane began its final descent toward Johnson City.

"What do you mean?" she asked hesitantly.

"What if you are wrong?" I continued. "What if there is a real heaven, a real hell, and a real Jesus whom you are rejecting as your only hope of heaven? What if when you die you stand before His throne and have to give an account of why you didn't believe? What if all your conclusions about who goes to heaven are wrong and what the Bible says is right?"

"I'm not wrong!" she defiantly proclaimed.

I continued, "Catherine, you told me yourself that you were an 'open-minded liberal' and that I was a 'close-minded Christian.' So if you are open-minded you must at the very least consider the possibility of your being wrong about this, otherwise you are not open-minded, you're just a liberal . . . and a close-minded one at that."

Her mouth dropped wide open. Up until then she had a comeback for every shred of evidence I laid before her. This time she had no snappy comeback. I must commend her for her honesty. She looked in my eyes and said, "What if I am wrong? I have never even thought about that possibility! What a good question! If I'm wrong, then I am going to hell!"

The last time I saw Catherine was at the baggage claim area in Johnson City, talking to her husband. I was close enough to overhear her say, "Honey, what if we are wrong about all this stuff that we believe?" Seeds of doubt were sown in the hope that the flower of faith would soon sprout, bloom, and transform.

The bottom line is this: We don't have *all* the answers as

Christians, but we do have *some,* and we do have a handful of great questions. Let's use them in love to get people to think about the biggest and most important issues in life!

THE 1 STATEMENT

Now that you've learned The 4 Questions, it's time to master The 1 Statement. I've found this statement to be a kind of get-out-of-jail-free card when it comes to having to know all of the answers. What is it?

That's a great question. I don't know, but I'll try to find out. Let's meet again soon.

Here's how it works. Somebody asks you a question about why you believe what you believe and you don't have the answer. What do you do? Do you make something up? No, that would be lying. You buy some time by using the statement, "That's a great question. I don't know, but I'll try to find out. Let's meet again soon." It gives you time to go back to your Bible, youth leader, or pastor to find an answer. You can also surf around www.dare2share.org to try to find the answer to your question. If you can't find the answer there you can always e-mail info@dare2share.org and an

Be careful. A surgeon doesn't use only a scalpel. A good surgeon uses clamps, clips, sponges, and an assortment of other surgical instruments. The scalpel is used to make cuts; a lot of the rest of the instruments are used to stop the bleeding. Make sure you use these questions appropriately as you cut into another person's belief system, and use a lot of love and listening skills to help stop the bleeding.

answer will be e-mailed back to you within a week.

Not only does this statement give you time to find an answer, it also uses the magic words that every Christian should learn, "I don't know!" It shows a bit of humility that is greatly needed in many Christian circles today. Too many times Christians act like know-it-alls when it comes to things eternal. Sure, there is a lot that we can know, a lot of stuff that is crystal clear from the Word of God. We can stand on that in humble confidence. But there is a lot we don't know and some stuff we can't know for sure. Maybe that's why Paul the apostle (who knew a lot of stuff) made it clear that there are many things we can't know on this side of eternity. Listen to his words in 1 Corinthians 13:12: "Now we see but a poor reflection as in a mirror; then we shall see face to face. Now I know in part; then I shall know fully, even as I am fully known."

Only when we are in heaven will we be able to be 100 percent sure about everything. Until then, we stand on the truths that we can know and we seek God's wisdom to begin the never-ending journey of learning more from God's Word and Spirit.

Believe it or not, the humility that is shown in not having all the answers on the spot may very well open the door for your friend to be receptive to hearing the gospel. Why? Because in a world drenched in arrogance, this kind of humility may be a stronger argument for the genuineness of Christianity than the best arguments in the world.

Another benefit of using this statement is that it helps you learn what I call Street Apologetics. What is this? It's the art of learning how to defend your faith one conversation at a time. The bottom line is that most of us aren't going to take a "How to Share the Gospel with Anyone from Any Cult, Philosophy, or World Religion" class that covers everything. Even if we did, there would be a lot that we would forget or not understand. But when you learn one conversation at a time, you tend not to forget those lessons. When you keep saying, "That's a great question! I don't know, but I'll find out. Let's meet again soon," you create a lifestyle of study and learning that goes deeper into your brain. You learn Street Apologetics, the unorthodox "street fighting" cousin of slick textbook apologetics.

I have never taken a class on apologetics. But I think I can defend my faith with the best of them. Why? I've learned with my friends, family, and strangers over decades of sharing Jesus with anyone and everyone.

The final benefit of using this statement is that it gives you an

CONFESSIONS

TRUE

When I was in high school I failed miserably at this. I wasn't competitive in sports due to an almost clinical lack of physical coordination. But I was, I'm sad to say, extremely competitive in all things spiritual, including sharing my faith. I hated not having the answers. There were times I so wanted to win the argument I'd make up facts (that's called lying) if need be, to convince them I was right. Two things happened as a result: 90 percent of the time they rejected Christ anyway. The old saying is right, "You can't argue somebody into the kingdom." And I lost my spiritual reward for those faith-sharing attempts. Even spiritual acts like sharing your faith don't get rewarded when done out of competitiveness or used with deceit. I thank the Lord that this was just a short fleshly phase in my life, and God taught me how to be honest when I didn't have the answer.

opportunity to continue the conversation. Remember that your goal is to take everyone you meet on that journey to Jesus. For some it's a shorter trip. For others it's a longer journey!

A PRAYER OF THANKSGIVING

Though merely saying a prayer never saved anybody from sin, leading others in prayer is a great way to help those who have put their faith in Christ for the first time to thank God for the free gift they just received. If you lead somebody through a prayer, make sure they know that saying the prayer doesn't get them into heaven; rather, it's simply a way for them to thank God for the free gift they just received through faith. The prayer should be short, simple, and clear. Maybe something like this:

> Dear God, thank You so much for forgiving all my sins through Jesus Christ. Through His death my sins are forgiven. Through His resurrection I have new life. Now that I have been forgiven, teach me to live a life that pleases You, not because I have to in order to get to heaven, but because I'm thankful that I am going to heaven. Amen.

A PRAYER OF THANKSGIVING

CHAPTER 21

KNOW HOW TO USE YOUR SEVEN SECRET "WEAPONS"

Years before Tom Cruise starred in the mega-hit *Mission Impossible* movies, there was a great TV show called *Mission Impossible*. Every week the same team of people pulled off the "impossible" by using all kinds of special technological gadgets. Every week the "impossible" became "possible"—it was not a question of "if" the special team was going to succeed but "how" they were going to do it.

God has not given us an impossible assignment. The evangelism mission is possible—but you must use the secret spiritual weapons at your disposal. What are these weapons and what are they for? The Bible tells us in 2 Corinthians 10:3-5:

> For though we live in the world, we do not wage war as the world does. The weapons we fight with are not the weapons of the world. On the contrary, they have divine power to demolish strongholds. We demolish arguments and every pretension that sets itself up against the knowledge of God, and we take captive every thought to make it obedient to Christ.

This Scripture passage says we are waging a war, not *on* our friends but *for* our friends. Our battle is against the Devil; we fight for the souls and minds of those around us who don't know Jesus. God has given us at least seven weapons we can use in sharing our faith that can help us defeat Satan and capture the hearts of everyone we know for Jesus!

1. Their Inner Knowledge of God

Everybody on the planet believes in God. Yes, even your atheist friends. Down deep inside secret chambers, there is the knowledge that one true God exists. Your friends may deny it. They may argue against it. But down deep inside they know He is there.

Listen to the words of Romans 1:18-22:

> The wrath of God is being revealed from heaven against all the godlessness and wickedness of men who suppress the truth by their wickedness, since what may be known about God is plain to them, because God has made it plain to them. For since the creation of the world God's invisible qualities—his eternal power and divine nature—have been clearly seen, being understood from what has been made, so that men are without excuse.
>
> For although they knew God, they neither glorified him as God nor gave thanks to him, but their thinking became futile and their foolish hearts were darkened. Although they claimed to be wise, they became fools.

What does this mean for you as you share Jesus with your friends? Assume that down deep inside they do believe in the existence of God. Keep talking as though there is a God and you will see them eventually using statements like, "Well, if God is so good then why does He allow suffering?" Questions like this show you that deep within they do believe in the existence of God and are just trying to find ways to push the truth away from themselves.

2. Their Personal Conscience
Everybody feels guilty when they do wrong. Why? God designed them that way! The Bible tells us in Romans 2:14-15:

> Indeed, when Gentiles, who do not have the law, do by nature things required by the law, they are a law for themselves, even though they do not have the law, since they show that the requirements of the law are written on their hearts, their consciences also bearing witness, and their thoughts now accusing, now even defending them.

As you talk to your friends, teammates, classmates, family, and coworkers about sin and how we all miss the mark of God's perfect standard, they will often feel guilty. Why? Because they have a conscience! It's important that you realize that not all guilt is bad. Some guilt comes from God. When people break one of God's commands or violate their conscience, they *should* feel guilty!

This feeling of guilt can lead to them recognizing their need for forgiveness from God. Check out "The Hammer and the Healer" section back in chapter 11 for a quick reminder on how you can use the law to get others to recognize their need for forgiveness.

3. The Power of the Word of God
The following two passages make it crystal clear that there is something internally powerful about God's Word. It is sharp like a

knife. When we listen to it, it can cut deeply into our consciences and expose us for what we really are. And it always accomplishes its goal, whether it be conviction or conversion.

> For the word of God is living and active. Sharper than any double-edged sword, it penetrates even to dividing soul and spirit, joints and marrow; it judges the thoughts and attitudes of the heart. Nothing in all creation is hidden from God's sight. Everything is uncovered and laid bare before the eyes of him to whom we must give account. (Hebrews 4:12-13)

◆

> So is my word that goes out from my mouth: It will not return to me empty, but will accomplish what I desire and achieve the purpose for which I sent it. (Isaiah 55:11)

What does this mean for you as you share your faith? Simply this: As you share the gospel with others, make sure that you quote and use verses from the Bible. If you don't know any verses, it's time to memorize a few. Here is a list of easy-to-memorize verses that I think every Christian teenager should know by heart:

> "For God so loved the world that he gave his one and only Son, that whoever believes in him shall not perish but have eternal life." (John 3:16)

◆

> "I tell you the truth, he who believes has everlasting life." (John 6:47)

◆

"And I will ask the Father, and he will give you another Counselor to be with you forever." (John 14:16)

◆

For all have sinned and fall short of the glory of God. (Romans 3:23)

◆

The wages of sin is death, but the gift of God is eternal life in Christ Jesus our Lord. (Romans 6:23)

◆

For it is by grace you have been saved, through faith—and this not from yourselves, it is the gift of God—not by works, so that no one can boast. (Ephesians 2:8-9)

◆

He saved us, not because of righteous things we had done, but because of his mercy. He saved us through the washing of rebirth and renewal by the Holy Spirit. (Titus 3:5)

Memorizing these verses will give you an "arsenal" to pick from when it comes to choosing the right verses to use at the right time. For help on how to memorize, reread "The 411" section near the beginning of chapter 15.

4. The Power of the Gospel

The gospel is like a kind of spiritual grenade. It is powerful. All you have to do is pull the pin, hurl it over their defenses, and duck! The shrapnel will penetrate into the soul, mind, and conscience of your nonbelieving friends. In Romans 1:16 Paul declared, "I am not ashamed of the gospel, because it is the power of God for the salvation of everyone who believes."

5. The Power of Prayer

"And pray for us, too, that God may open a door for our message" (Colossians 4:3).

It is God who creates our opportunities to share the gospel with those we encounter every single day. We must pray that God gives them open hearts and receptive minds. The power of prayer cannot be stopped. I heard this quote when I was 15 years old and have never forgotten it: "Satan laughs at our labor. He mocks all our plans. But he trembles when we pray." When you start praying, the hearts of your friends start to open and the knees of Satan start to shake.

Through your prayers the Spirit of God does His work as well. His job is to convict and convince. He convicts your friends of sin and convinces them that Jesus is who He claimed to be. Jesus reassures us in John 16:8 that when the Spirit of God comes, "he will convict the world of guilt in regard to sin and righteousness and judgment."

Your prayers unleash His power to convince and convict your friends. Pray for your friends, knowing that the Spirit of God can open their hearts to make them receptive to the gospel of Jesus!

WARNING!

Don't fall into the trap of thinking that you are in some battle of equally valid belief systems. The gospel is not just another idea. It is the greatest story ever told. This message is not philosophical speculation or just another religion. It is far from either. It is the truth. So share this powerful message in humble confidence knowing that it is the truth.

6. A Life of Doing Good

There is something powerful about a life of doing good deeds for other people. When Mother Teresa was alive, she earned the respect of the entire planet because of her lifelong sacrificial work in the streets of Calcutta, India. When you are always doing things for others, you too will earn a reputation throughout your school as someone who loves God and loves others. This reputation can open up the door for you to share Jesus in a powerful way.

Scripture says, "Neither do people light a lamp and put it under a bowl. Instead they put it on its stand, and it gives light to everyone in the house. In the same way, let your light shine before men, that they may see your good deeds and praise your Father in heaven" (Matthew 5:15-16).

Here are some ideas that can get you started doing some good deeds:

- Buy lunch for someone you don't know (or do know but don't hang with) at school.
- Write notes of encouragement to those who seem down
- Help others with their homework.
- Take time to listen.
- Sit with somebody during lunch you don't know well and get to know him or her.
- Coordinate a school-wide canned food drive for a local rescue mission.
- Coordinate a neighborhood cleanup.
- Get a group of teenagers from your school to visit a retirement center on a Saturday just to talk to the elderly and encourage them.

The list of possibilities is almost endless. The point is to start living a life of good deeds and let your little light shine!

7. Your Love for Other Christians

"By this all men will know that you are my disciples, if you love one another" (John 13:35).

Jesus told His followers that they had something to prove to the watching world. What was it? That they were fully surrendered followers of Jesus! How did they prove this 2,000 years ago? Not by wearing a Christian toga T-shirt or by having some religious slogan on the bumper sticker on their chariot. They proved it by the sacrificial love they had for each other.

There's something powerful, almost mystical, about the way a group of Christians who are empowered by the Spirit of God care about each other. Their sacrificial service, attitude of respect, and true affection that they have for each other can be a huge influence on the watching world.

Have you experienced this kind of deep friendship with a group of Christians on your campus? If not, it's time to begin to pursue that depth of relationship with the spiritually on-fire Christians on your campus. Meet together to pray and encourage each other weekly. Let others see your love for one another. It will make an impact in ways you can't even begin to imagine.

A FINAL WORD ABOUT YOUR SECRET WEAPONS

As you share your faith, just remember you are entering this battle with Satan for the souls of your friends with an unfair advantage. Your weapons have power to convince, convict, and transform. The apostle Paul recognized these weapons. In 2 Corinthians 6:7

he noted he served God "in truthful speech and in the power of God; with weapons of righteousness in the right hand and in the left." Satan, however, is battling with the obsolete weapons of the same age-old lies. Trust in God's Word and God's Spirit to do their work of transformation as you share the greatest message on the planet.

CHAPTER 22

HOW TO HELP NEW BELIEVERS GROW IN THEIR RELATIONSHIP WITH JESUS

When a friend, family member, teammate, classmate, or stranger puts his or her faith and trust in Jesus Christ, it is an absolute miracle. They are transformed and transferred—transformed from a child of the Devil (John 8:44) to a child of God (John 1:12) and transferred out of the kingdom of darkness into the kingdom of God (Colossians 1:13).

So what comes next? They must be brought into a local church and trained in the basics of living their newfound faith!

Can you imagine a doctor bringing a newborn baby into this world, cleaning it off, wrapping it in a warm blanket, and then throwing it into a trash can? Of course not! The baby is kept warm, clean, and fed. The goal is that the brand-new baby grows with just the right amount of rest and nutrition and love.

What's true of newborn babies in the earthly realm is true in the spiritual realm as well. When we were "born again" into the family of God, we needed every bit as much warmth and nutrition and love as a new baby does. The reason you are reading this book to begin with is because somebody took care of you after you became a child of God and helped you grow into a healthy, thriving Christian.

So how do you help newborn babies in Jesus grow into spiritually developed believers? There are three things we need to give them: shelter, nutrition, and lots and lots of love.

1. Shelter
More than anything a new believer needs shelter. This is a warm place where he or she can grow and thrive. What is it for a new believer? It is a local church! This incubator of care is where the newborn believers find the warmth and security they need to grow spiritually. If you have the privilege of bringing somebody into the kingdom of God, take him or her to church and youth group with you! Without church, new believers could spiritually freeze and die.

2. Nutrition
When somebody comes into the family of God they need the spiritual food that is going to help them grow into healthy Christians. This nutrition comes from the Bible. It is the basic stuff of Christianity. Answers to questions like who God is, can the Bible be

---

Dare 2 Share Ministries has developed a Web site resource with new and growing believers in mind. Go to www.dare2share.org and sign yourself and your friends up to receive a free weekly resource called "Soul Fuel." This weekly devotional training will be e-mailed to you and your friends from that moment on. Each Soul Fuel tackles one of the 30 core truths of Christianity in a real, relevant, and teen-friendly way. Alert your youth leader and parents to the accompanying resources for them to use on this Web site as well. Best of all, it's all FREE!

trusted, and how do I share my faith are all important in the basic nutrition package.

When a newborn baby comes into the world the most basic nutrition is received almost exclusively from his or her mother's milk. This milk provides nutrients to make the baby strong and enzymes to prevent sickness and disease in those crucial early months. In the same way, the Bible describes itself as this kind of mother's milk for every believer: "Like newborn babies, crave pure spiritual milk, so that by it you may grow up in your salvation, now that you have tasted that the Lord is good" (1 Peter 2:2-3).

3. Lots and Lots of love

Love is the warm blanket that wraps these newborn babies. It is the tender, loving care of spiritual fathers and mothers who look after, rock, kiss, and hold the newborn. It's how Paul loved new believers. He writes to them, "We were gentle among you, like a mother caring for her little children. We loved you so much that we were delighted to share with you not only the gospel of God but our lives as well, because you had become so dear to us" (1 Thessalonians 2:7-8).

How do we love new believers? We serve them. We listen to them. We help them learn to take those first few steps of obedience from baptism to discovering their very own spiritual gifts to learning how to share their faith with others. In this whole exciting process we must be patient and somewhat pushy at the same time. We love them enough to accept them as they are, but we also love them enough not to leave them there.

Just as any baby goes through different phases of development, from being able to roll over to learning to crawl and then walk, new believers must be encouraged to make spiritual progress as well. We are there like a mom and dad encouraging them to take that next step, picking them up when they fall and cheering them on again.

Do your best to follow up every single person you bring to Jesus. Get these newborns food, shelter, and love.

When it comes to convincing new believers of the importance of not only attending church but also serving Christ with all of their hearts, I have found "The Million-Dollar Question" to be very useful.

Once someone indicates faith in Jesus and I am convinced that they understand the gospel message, I use this powerful question, "If I were to give you a million dollars right now, would you slap me and walk away?" Their answer usually goes something like, "Of course not." When I probe a little deeper and ask why, they answer something like, "Because I would be grateful for your tremendous gift!" Then I ask them another question: "God has just given you something of infinitely more value than a million dollars. He has given you eternal life! Are you going to slap Him in the face and walk away or are you going to serve Him?" Every time their answer is "serve Him." "Why?" I ask. "Because I am grateful for His tremendous gift to me" is usually their response.

The power of The Million Dollar Question is that it enables the new believer to understand that the reason we serve Jesus Christ is not a "have to" but a "want to." We serve Jesus not to prove, keep, or earn our salvation but because of it! Wholehearted service to God flows out of a thankful heart. The Million Dollar Question helps new believers get started with just that!

SHARE

YOUR GUIDE

TO

SHARING

YOUR

FAITH WITH

ANYONE

PART THREE

CHAPTER 23

STARBUCKS SPIRITUALITY

Right now as I sit in a Starbucks drinking a venti, sugar-free, vanilla, extra-shot Americano, I am reminded of a skit I wrote.

The drama opens with a line of people waiting to get their fix, but instead of customized caffeine concoctions, theirs was a have-it-your-way religious fix. One would order a *Carmel Cult Latte* with a *Hare Krishna Cookie* on the side. The next customer would be torn between the *Tai Chi Chai* and the *Mormon Frappaccino* (decaf only).

The only drink that wasn't served at this particular spirituality shop was a *Venti Jesus*. Your actualized, open-minded barista was open to giving you a quasi Jesus (Jesus with a shot of something else) but not a straight-up Jesus. Why? Because once you had Him you would never thirst again. He was *the* way, *the* truth, *the* life, *the* drink.

Once you taste of Jesus, not only do you never thirst again, but you become suddenly possessed with a desire to get others to try this drink out. And if that happens too often, then Spiritual Starbucks is out of business for good.

This skit had a strong point that resonated with teens. Their world mixes spiritual beliefs like Starbucks mixes lattes, customized to their personal specifications. And that's a problem. Why? Because it assumes that it doesn't matter what you believe, only that you truly believe in *something*. If that's true, then maybe we are too hard on the villains of history. For instance, Hitler truly believed in something. His atrocities were simply natural outgrowths of what he sincerely believed.

If it doesn't matter what we believe, only that we believe, then morality is up for grabs depending on one's latte order. If you order an *Atheist Americano,* where morality is irrelevant because we are the random results of an endless series of evolutionary mutations, then why not rape, murder, and pillage?

But if we were made in the image of God for the glory of God, and if that same God who created us died for us and rose for us and lives in us, then why wouldn't we make it our life goal to make the world a better place? Why wouldn't we seek to honor those around us, even those who believe something radically different, because they too were made by God and for God? Why wouldn't we spend the rest of our lives serving Jesus in all His richness and taste to all those we come in contact with every day?

As I type these words a line is forming at Starbucks. It reminds me of how many people love the taste of coffee. How much more would people love the taste of Jesus if they would simply try Him out. What's more, Jesus never charges. He paid the price completely on the cross. Every other religion and belief system comes with a hefty charge, whether it be obeying some list of regulations, stopping some habit, starting some mantra, whatever. But this latte of life eternal is free, prepurchased with the blood of the barista.

And before He rose into heaven He gave us the charge to go into all the world and open up Jesus Latte franchises everywhere.

He called us to be *Bible Baristas* and to raise up an army of baristas-in-training out of all nations. He commanded us to baptize them into this reality with three shots of transformation—the Father, Son, and Holy Spirit. And He reminded us that He will be right at our side as we stand behind the counter of political incorrectness delivering Jesus in all of His strength to a world in desperate need of better taste.

What does all this mean as you share your faith with all your friends who hang out at Spiritual Starbucks? Realize their beliefs are probably a blended drink . . . a shot of Jesus and a few pumps of New Age or whatever.

Help them understand what Jesus meant when He said, "I am the way and the truth and the life. No one can come to the Father except through me" (John 14:6).

"Venti Jesus, please!"

◆ ◆ ◆

What religious beliefs are your friends concocting their spiritual latte from? Just having a basic understanding of the belief systems your friends may be choosing from can help you reach out to them and have L³ conversations. The next 14 chapters describe belief systems you may encounter at school, at the mall, online, at the gym, or anywhere people hang out and talk about life. All of the personal stories in the following chapters are true stories, though in some cases people's names and certain details of their stories have been changed to protect the privacy of the individuals involved. These stories are not meant to stereotype or degrade any certain group. I offer them to you as a way to personalize these belief systems and allow you to benefit from my own experience of sharing my faith in Jesus with others. Remember that some of those you encounter may take their latte straight up while others may be combining a shot of this and a few pumps of that to concoct their own special blend of spirituality. So ask questions, listen carefully, and customize your dialogue to fit each individual.

CHAPTER 24

ALISHA
THE AGNOSTIC

Alisha is a friend of a friend. She is smart and knows the Bible extremely well. Although she had a pretty religious background, she'd been in trouble with the law over the last few years for drugs and such. In her house growing up, she had to abide by a whole bunch of rules but was not taught about having an intimate relationship with God. This and some other influences caused her to rebel. Eventually her rebellion led to agnosticism.

As I shared with Alisha again and again, she was very open to discussion. She shared with me her doubts about God, Jesus, the Bible—everything that she had been raised to believe and embrace. She became more and more receptive to the gospel but still has a whole lot of questions. I'm still communicating with her and praying that she will come to embrace the real Christ, not the religious Jesus that her parents pushed on her. I pray she'll come to know the real, relevant, and powerful Jesus of the Bible!

Basic Description
Alisha the Agnostic feels that God's existence can't be proven or disproven based on available evidence. For Alisha to believe in God or any kind of deity, she would need logical and rational proof. This is what makes Alisha different from Andy the Atheist (see chapter 25): She would most likely be open to the idea of God's existence if sufficient proof is offered. Alisha is similar to Andy in that they both deny the existence of a heaven/hell/spiritual world. Alisha would definitely not consider her agnostic beliefs a "religion," but rather she would say they are concepts.

Common Misconceptions
- Alisha's group is the same as atheists.
- Alisha's beliefs come from being an indecisive, unintelligent person.
- Alisha's beliefs are a compromise between believing/not believing in God.

Three Fascinating Facts
- The word "agnostic" literally means "without knowledge." What it means is that there is insufficient knowledge to "prove" there is a God.
- The title "agnostic" was coined by a famous English biologist named Thomas Huxley.
- For many years it was illegal to be an agnostic in France, and for this crime a person would receive the death sentence.

Things We Probably Agree On
- Alisha believes that much truth can be discovered.
- Alisha believes that people should treat each other with fairness and justice.
- Alisha believes in being a good person.

Things We Probably Disagree On
- Alisha wants irrefutable proof for the existence of God, whereas God requires that we have faith in Him (Hebrews 11:1-3).
- Alisha believes that all people are born basically good, whereas the Bible teaches that all people are born with a predisposition toward sin (Psalm 51:5).

- Alisha does not believe in hell, but thinks there could be some kind of heaven, whereas the Bible teaches the existence of both heaven and hell (Matthew 3:16; Luke 12:5).

Suggested Conversation Starters
- What would "proof" for God's existence look like to you?
- Are there things you believe in that have not been proven to you?
- Have you ever thought about the possibility that you might be wrong? (Be ready to answer this question yourself!)

A Compliment to Use
- I really appreciate your honest questions. Too many times Christians aren't honest enough to ask the harder questions about life and God.

Interesting Quotes
- "I don't know & you don't either."—militant agnostic, bumper sticker
- "I do not consider it an insult, but rather a compliment to be called an agnostic. I do not pretend to know where many ignorant men are sure—that is all that agnosticism means."—Clarence Darrow at the Scopes trial, 1925[1]

Other Tips/Suggestions
- Try and stick to the issue of what "proof" is for God and how He has made Himself known through creation and science.
- Agnostics tend to look at Christians as intellectually inferior, so be sure to have your ideas and discussion points well thought out.

- Christians sometimes come across as superior to agnostics, so be sure to maintain a respectful and gracious attitude.

For Further Research
- www.dare2share.org/agnostics
- *The Case for Christ: Student Edition* by Lee Strobel

ANDY THE
ATHEIST

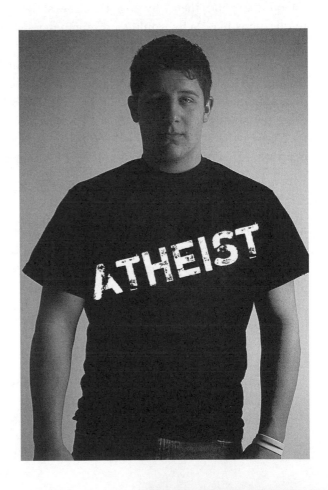

I met Andy on a camping trip in the mountains (see chapter 8). Out of the seven students we took, Andy was among the most vocal. A devout atheist, he had been raised in a family that didn't go to church or believe in God. His arguments ranged from "Well, if God is so good, then why does He allow suffering in the world?" to questions like "Why would God send a devout Muslim to hell just because he didn't believe in Jesus?"

While I answered Andy straight from the Bible, he didn't trust in Christ as his Savior that week. He did, however, by his own admission "come closer" than he ever had before to considering the possibility that God exists. Andy is reading *The Case for Christ* by Lee Strobel and is keeping an open mind to the possibility that God could exist and that Christianity could be true.

Pray for Andy to believe.

Basic Description

Andy does not believe in the existence of God, a supreme being, or any other spiritual beings for that matter. In his opinion this physical universe has always existed, and when a person dies, he or she ceases to exist forever. Andy most likely finds meaning in life through relationships and accomplishments.

Common Misconceptions

- Andy hates or strongly dislikes all Christians.
- Andy hasn't thought through his position.
- Because Andy doesn't believe in God, he necessarily feels purposeless and lives immorally.

Three Fascinating Facts
- Andy's group has founded organizations such as The Freedom from Religion Foundation and Internet Infidels.
- Andy's group (on average) has a higher level of education than the general population.
- Andy's group once had a man named C. S. Lewis in it who later became a Christian and wrote *The Chronicles of Narnia* series and many other great books.

Things We Probably Agree On
- Andy believes in the basic value of all people.
- Andy believes that relationships are important.
- Andy believes that no one person has all the answers.

Things We Probably Disagree On
- Andy does not believe that the Bible is the Word of God, whereas the Bible claims to be just that (2 Timothy 3:16) and proves this claim through hundreds of fulfilled prophecies (Acts 3:18).
- Andy does not believe God exists, whereas the Bible clearly affirms His existence (Exodus 3:14).
- Andy does not believe in heaven or hell, whereas the Bible teaches the existence of both (Matthew 3:16; Luke 12:5).

Suggested Conversation Starters
- Why have you chosen to not believe in the existence of God?
- Could you be open to the possibility that a God exists?

- Do you think there is a difference between religion and a relationship with God? Why or why not?

A Compliment to Use

- I appreciate the courage you must have in your heart. I don't think that I could face life and all of its hardships without belief in a loving and all-powerful God.

Interesting Quotes

- "Give a man a fish, and you'll feed him for a day; give him a religion, and he'll starve to death while praying for a fish."— Timothy Jones[1]
- "It may be that our role on this planet is not to worship God, but to create him."—Arthur C. Clarke[2]
- "I'm sickened by all religions. Religion has divided people. I don't think there's any difference between the pope wearing a large hat and parading around with a smoking purse and an African painting his face white and praying to a rock."— Howard Stern[3]

Other Tips/Suggestions

- This is perhaps the most difficult faith-sharing scenario in the world, so you will need to spend some time finding common ground and defining your terms.
- Oftentimes when talking to atheists they will "forget" that they don't believe in the existence of God. They'll say things like, "Well, if God is so good then why . . ." Gently point out to them that according to Romans 1:18-22 everybody, down deep inside, believes in the existence of God but they

push down that truth and try to deny it with human rationalizations.

- One of the key issues when sharing with an atheist is to establish that the Bible is God's Word, so be sure you can walk him or her through the evidences for this fact. As well, atheists love to point out all the "contradictions" in the Bible, so be careful not to get too sidetracked on this issue. The other key issue is the birth, death, and resurrection of Jesus Christ, so (again) be sure you have a thought-out line of reasoning when discussing this.

For Further Research
- www.dare2share.org/atheists
- *The Case for Christ: Student Edition* by Lee Strobel

CHAPTER 26

BAILEY THE BUDDHIST

In the process of writing this book, I realized that my life journey hasn't brought me into contact with very many Buddhists. Last weekend as I was catching a flight from one speaking engagement to the next, I prayed to God that I would meet a Buddhist on my coming flight. Arriving at my assigned seat, a young lady was getting situated nearby. In the course of our conversation during the flight, I shared with her that I was writing a book for teenagers. I explained how I was going to share about different religions, and Bailey volunteered that she was raised in a Buddhist family. Because we weren't sitting right next to each other, it was difficult to carry on the conversation. But she was definitely open. I gave her my e-mail address and asked her to connect with me online where I could find out more about her Buddhist background and beliefs. I let her know that I was looking forward to hearing her beliefs and sharing my beliefs with her via e-mail. My challenge is this: How do I convince her that the gospel message is the truth, especially when she was raised in a strictly Buddhist home? The conversation continues . . .

Basic Description

While Bailey was raised in a strict Buddhist home, many American Buddhists can best be summed up by the term "religious atheist" because the American form of Buddhism is perfect for those who reject the idea of God yet still seek after the history and tradition of religious experience. Buddhism also includes a strong emphasis on meditation, which gives its followers a sense of inner peace. A Buddhist's ultimate goal is to achieve nirvana (not the band)— which is a state of being that is totally separated from individuality, negative emotions, and desires. The reason Buddhists seek this is because these things cause suffering and evil in the world, and force people into an endless cycle of birth/death/rebirth with bad karma. Buddhism answers the question of suffering and evil in the world very simply: Bad people do bad things, so they pay for it in subsequent lives (i.e., karma).

Buddhists do not believe in a personal God, so there is no "church" or worship in Buddhism. Also, the concepts of forgiveness, heavenly hope, and final judgment are absent from Buddhism as well. It's helpful to think of their worldview more as a philosophy than a "religion."

Common Misconceptions
- Buddhists believe that Buddha was God.
- Buddhists worship in a temple.
- Buddhists have a big belly and if you rub it you'll have good luck.

Three Fascinating Facts
- Buddha himself was unsure about what happens after death.
- Many so-called "sayings" of Buddha were actually written four hundred years after his death.
- The term "nirvana" literally means the "blowing out" of existence.

Things We Probably Agree On
- Buddhists seek inner peace.
- Buddhists believe in life after death.
- Buddhists are troubled by evil and suffering in the world.

Things We Probably Disagree On
- Buddhists do not believe in a personal God, whereas the Bible teaches not only His existence, but His personal concern as well (Psalm 46:10).
- Buddhists believe in a repeated cycle of birth/death/rebirth, whereas the Bible teaches that we die only once, then face judgment for how we lived our lives (Hebrews 9:27).
- Buddhists believe that Buddha showed the path to "salvation" (i.e., nirvana), whereas the Bible teaches that Jesus is the only way to heaven (John 14:6).

Suggested Conversation Starters
- What do you believe about what happens after death?
- Why is there evil and suffering in the world?
- Have you ever felt the need to be forgiven?

A Compliment to Use
- One of the things I really appreciate about Buddhism is how it seeks peace. We have too much war and conflict in the world and not nearly enough peace.

Interesting Quotes
- "Things are not what they appear to be: nor are they otherwise."—Buddha, Surangama Sutra[1]
- "The ultimate authority must always rest with the individual's own reason and critical analysis."—H. H., the 14th Dalai Lama[2]

Other Tips/Suggestions

- Keep in mind that there are several different "versions" of Buddhism, so make sure you get a detailed explanation from your Buddhist friends about what they believe and why they believe it.
- Since Buddhists seek to experience salvation (nirvana) through a system of good deeds, make sure you explain that biblical salvation is a free gift received through faith in Jesus based on His death, burial, and resurrection.
- Because many Buddhists are Asian or of Asian descent, you need to be sensitive toward the cultural differences that may exist. If you aren't, it will be difficult to establish a friendship with them, and as a result, it will be more complicated to share your faith.

For Further Research

- www.dare2share.org/buddhists
- *Sharing Your Faith with a Buddhist* by M. S. Thirumalai, Madasamy Thirumalai

CHAPTER 27

ERIN THE EVOLUTIONIST

When I met Erin, she was an exemplary high school student. Pretty soon we were in a conversation about spiritual things, and she wanted to argue. Specifically she wanted to debate over evolution. Although I knew a lot about the creation/evolution debate, I decided to avoid the subject altogether and just stick with sharing the gospel.

As Erin spouted "fact" after fact at me, I kept saying things like, "That's really interesting, Erin, but God isn't going to ask you about evolution when you stand before Him. He's going to ask you about what you believed about Jesus." After about 30 minutes or so of talking, Erin finally exclaimed, "Greg, you are a great debater!" I replied, "Erin, I haven't even argued with you. I have simply shared the message of Jesus! The Spirit of God is convicting your soul that what I'm saying is true. The Spirit of God is winning the argument in your heart!"

Basic Description

Erin and her group are very similar to Andy the Atheist and his belief system—in fact there is incredible overlap. The way to distinguish the two groups is as follows: All (or nearly all) atheists are evolutionists, but not all evolutionists are atheists. There are some (called theistic evolutionists or progressive creationists) who believe God used evolution in the process of creating and sustaining life. Erin, however, is not in this group. She is an atheistic evolutionist—meaning she believes that all life on earth came as a result of random chance. In her view, there is no God or spiritual world, because the universe has always been here (i.e., matter is eternal), and when you combine time and chance, anything can happen—even such things as life from nonliving materials, and personality from nonpersonal organisms.

Common Misconceptions
- Erin thinks that morals don't matter because we all evolved.
- Erin doesn't think there are some hard-to-explain shortcomings with the evolutionary theory.
- Erin has thought through the implications of accepting atheistic evolution as the explanation for the origin of life.

Three Fascinating Facts
- Charles Darwin had aspirations of becoming a pastor, but lost his faith after the death of his daughter.
- The theory of evolution rests heavily on the existence of transitional fossils ("the missing link"), but so far none have been discovered.
- Evolutionists and Creationists are both working with the same evidence; the issue is how a person interprets the evidence (for example, is the possibility of God real or not?).

Things We Probably Agree On
- Erin believes that life and nature are incredibly complex.
- Erin believes that any statement about reality should have some level of proof.
- Erin believes that in the beginning there was a big event that led to all life as we know it.

Things We Probably Disagree On
- Erin does not believe in God, whereas the Bible teaches that the proof for God lies in creation itself (Psalm 19:1-3; Romans 1:18-20).

- Erin's beliefs are based solely on scientific "evidence," whereas the Bible teaches that our beliefs about the origins of the universe need to have a level of faith (Hebrews 11:3).
- Erin believes truth and morality are subjectively determined by society and common sense, whereas the Bible teaches that truth and morality are constant and absolute because they are determined by God's inspired Word (Matthew 24:35; 2 Timothy 3:16-17).

Suggested Conversation Starters
- What led you to believe that life and the universe happened by chance?
- Did you know that scientific evidence backs up the creation account in Genesis? (Direct them to www.answersingenesis. org for further research in this area.)
- If there truly is a God who created us, how would that affect your view of what happens when we die?

A Compliment to Use
- I am in awe how evolutionists work so hard and diligently to prove their position. Evolutionists seem to be very intelligent, hardworking, and determined.

Interesting Quotes
- "The number of intermediate varieties, which have formerly existed on the earth, (must) be truly enormous. Why then is not every geological formation and every stratum full of such intermediate links? Geology assuredly does not reveal any such finely graduated organic chain; and this, perhaps,

is the most obvious and gravest objection which can be urged against my theory."—Charles Darwin, *The Origin of Species*[1]

- "I love fools' experiments. I am always making them."—Charles Darwin[2]

Other Tips/Suggestions

- Don't get bogged down too much in arguments over the science of creation/evolution; rather, focus on evidence for the existence of God in nature.
- Many evolutionists see Christians as weak individuals who only believe in God because they need a crutch. Because of this, try and focus on how your relationship with God has actually set you free to become who you were intended to be in the first place.
- Point out the weaknesses of the evolutionist's worldview in terms of morality being determined by "common sense" and society. By doing this, the evolutionist may see the need for absolute truth/morality—and therefore a God.

For Further Research

- www.dare2share.org/evolutionists
- *The Case for a Creator—Student Edition* by Lee Strobel and Jane Vogel

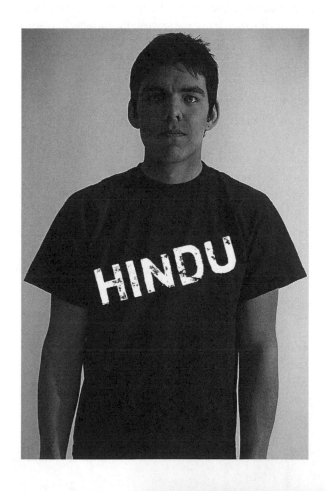

CHAPTER 28

HARI THE HINDU

I met Hari while on a mission trip to India. He was a student at a Catholic school, although not Catholic himself. He had always been a Hindu. All of his family and most of his friends are Hindu. He had always heard that the poverty in his life was a result of karma (what goes around comes around) from his past lives. As a result of this karma mentality, he didn't get a lot of compassion from those around him who had more money. In their minds he was just reaping what he had sown in a past life.

Hari worshipped cows and cobras as sacred. He hungered for the meat from the cow that he bowed down to worship, but couldn't eat it. Nor could he kill the cobras that he encountered from time to time. (He had to call his Muslim friend to come and kill them!) Both cow and cobra and countless other animals, rodents, and entities were gods to him, although the ultimate god was nothingness . . . and that was his ultimate aspiration!

When I shared with Hari that there was a God who loved him enough to send His Son to die for him, he was immediately interested. To know that God loved him in spite of his poverty and the sin in his life was an awakening. To hear that Jesus was slaughtered for him on the cross and that He rose again to offer him eternal life blew Hari away!

Hari trusted in Jesus and was rejected by his family, cut off as a heretic. He is now plugged into a Campus Crusade group in Bangalore, India, where he is growing in his faith and sharing Christ with all of his Hindu friends.

Basic Description

Hinduism originated in India over three thousand years ago, and over the years it has developed into an extremely complex and complicated religion. There are, however, several concepts that Hindus would most likely agree on.

Hindus believe that the nature of ultimate reality (called Brahman) is impersonal, and that all humans in their true selves (called Atman) are simply an extension of that reality. In other words, we are all a part of the impersonal nature of the universe (i.e., Atman is Brahman).

Hindus feel that humanity's biggest problem is that we have forgotten or are ignorant of our divine nature, which is why we try to define ourselves as individuals and feel the need for material possessions. Because of this problem, our destiny is to go through a series of reincarnations (i.e., an ever-revolving wheel of life, death, and rebirth), which are affected by good and bad karma until we realize that our separate self is just an illusion and become one with Brahman.

So in other words, life is an illusion where we mistakenly believe we are individuals. The amount of good and bad we do in each life determines the state of the next. For example, if I am a bad person I might be reincarnated as a dung beetle; if I am good, I might come back as a sacred animal like a cow or a more spiritually enlightened human. The goal for Hindus is to eventually not consider themselves as individuals anymore—rather an extension of the impersonal nature of ultimate reality.

Common Misconceptions

- Hindus don't believe in one supreme God. (Even though they have many gods in their belief system, they claim to believe in one supreme God.)

- Hindus are pacifists and have a deeper level of spiritual peace than most people.
- Hindus hold the same beliefs as Buddhists.

Three Fascinating Facts
- There are more than 300 million gods in Hinduism (although one impersonal supreme being).
- Hindus believe Jesus was an example of the one supreme God taking a human form (called an avatar).
- The main sacred books Hindus use are called the Upanishads.

Things We Probably Agree On
- Hindus believe in one supreme God.
- Hindus believe that Jesus Christ existed.
- Hindus seek salvation in the afterlife.

Things We Probably Disagree On
- Hindus believe that the one supreme God is impersonal, whereas the Bible teaches that God has a personal name and a personality (Exodus 3:14-15).
- Hindus believe in reincarnation, whereas the Bible teaches that people only die once (Hebrews 9:27) and then face judgment (Revelation 20:11-15).
- Hindus believe that Jesus was just one of many earthly appearances of the one supreme God who comes in the forms of people and animals, whereas the Bible teaches that Jesus is the only appearance of God in the flesh (John 1:1-5).

Suggested Conversation Starters
- Do all religions/paths lead to God? Why or why not?

- Have you ever thought through the implications of whether the Bible is true and Hinduism is a false religion?
- What do you believe about Jesus Christ?

A Compliment to Use

- Hinduism is a religion that has stood the test of time. There are a lot of nice, hardworking people who are a part of its rich tradition.

Interesting Quotes

- "When the five senses and the mind are still, and the reasoning intellect rests in silence, then begins the highest path."—Upanishads, the Hindu sacred writings[1]
- "By meditation on Him, by contemplation of Him, and by communion with Him, there comes in the end destruction of earthly delusion."—Upanishads[2]

Other Tips/Suggestions

- Don't expect every Hindu to believe the same things, so make sure you let your Hindu friend clearly express his or her views.
- Stay away from unclear terms like "born again" and "saved," because the Hindu will define them in terms of Hindu belief (i.e., born again = reincarnation, saved = one with Brahman).
- Work very hard on the relationship with your Hindu friend.

For Further Research

- www.dare2share.org/hindus
- *Sharing Your Faith with a Hindu* by M. S. Thirumalai, Madasamy Thirumalai

CHAPTER 29

JORDAN THE JEHOVAH'S WITNESS

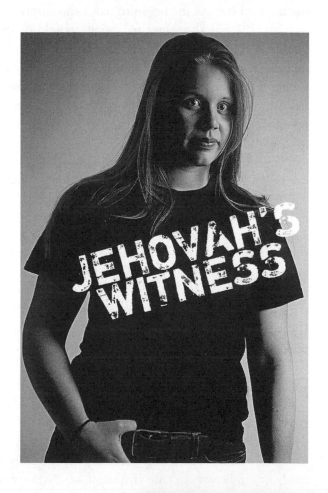

I met Jordan at my door. She was not alone but had another lady with her, an older lady. It was hard to shut the door because she also had a little child with her. At first it felt like she brought the child along to get some sympathy from me so that I wouldn't shut the door on her. As she began to talk I was impressed at her boldness and the way she asked me about eternal life. But being thoroughly acquainted with her beliefs, I began to ask questions about heaven (I knew she believed that heaven was only for a select group of 144,000 individuals) and hell (I knew she believed that hell was not eternal, but a place where sinners are literally incinerated in an instant). Although the questions were tough, I tried to ask them in a nice way.

Once the questions started getting tougher, the older lady with her began to jump in. It became obvious to me that this older lady was training Jordan, and when it got too tough, she would take over. So I simply asked the older lady to allow Jordan and me to continue the conversation; after all, Jordan was the one who began the conversation, not her. The older lady didn't want to hear that, but I insisted. As Jordan and I continued our conversation, it became clear that she didn't have good responses to my many questions. Finally, the older lady said something like, "Jordan, this man is not willing to listen to the truth. Let's go." Hesitantly, she complied. But I could tell that in the midst of our conversations there were many new thoughts in Jordan's mind, new doubts about the validity of the belief system that she had been embracing.

Basic Description

Jordan's group is called the Jehovah's Witnesses and has been around for more than a hundred years. In the early 1870s, a Bible study group began in Pennsylvania; it was led by a man named

Charles Taze Russell. In July 1879, the first issue of the magazine *Zion's Watch Tower and Herald of Christ's Presence* appeared. By 1880 dozens of congregations had spread from that one small Bible study into nearby states. In 1881, Zion's Watchtower Tract Society was formed. The Society's name was later changed to Watchtower Bible and Tract Society. Many were witnessing from house to house offering Bible literature. Fifty persons were doing this full time in 1888; now the average number worldwide is about 700,000. Jehovah's Witnesses identify themselves as Christian and number over six million.[1] Their headquarters are in New York. It is an international organization known for its extensive preaching and publishing activities, with *The Watchtower* and *Awake!* religious magazines and the *New World Translation of the Holy Scriptures* being the most popular examples.

Common Misconceptions
- Jordan uses the same Bible as Christians.
- Jordan's group is just like the Mormons because they go door-to-door.
- Jordan's group is a subgroup of Christianity.

Three Fascinating Facts
- Jordan goes to Jehovah's Witnesses meetings five times per week.
- Jordan does not celebrate Thanksgiving, Christmas, or birthdays, nor does she say "bless you" when you sneeze.
- Jordan can't get a blood transfusion for religious reasons.

Things We Probably Agree On
- Jordan believes there is one true God, Jehovah.

- Jordan believes in a real person named Jesus Christ.
- Jordan believes Christ died for our sins.

Things We Probably Disagree On
- Jordan doesn't believe in the Trinity (the biblical concept that we serve one God who exists in the form of three unique persons, the Father, Son, and Holy Spirit) or an eternal hell, whereas the Bible teaches the Trinity (Deuteronomy 6:4; 1 Peter 1:2; John 1:1-3; Acts 5:3-4) and a literal hell (Revelation 14:10-11; 20:15).
- Jordan doesn't believe Jesus is God in the flesh; rather, He is the same person in the Bible as the archangel Michael, whereas the Bible teaches He is God in the flesh (John 1:1-3, 14).
- Jordan doesn't believe eternal life is received by grace through faith alone, whereas the Bible does (Ephesians 2:8-9).

Suggested Conversation Starters
- Are you ever worried by the reality that Jehovah's Witnesses' beliefs are so out of line with what so many other churches believe?
- What if there really is an eternal hell where those who don't trust Christ go for eternity?
- Why do you think that Jesus claimed the personal name of Jehovah ("I am") as His own in John 8:58? Could it be that He Himself was Jehovah?

A Compliment to Use
- One of the things I really appreciate about Jehovah's Witnesses is how dedicated they are to knowing what they believe and sharing what they believe with others.

Interesting Quotes

- "It should be expected that the Lord would have a means of communication to his people on the earth, and he has clearly shown that the magazine called *The Watchtower* is used for that purpose."—*1939 Yearbook of Jehovah's Witnesses*[2]
- "Jesus never claimed to be God. Everything he said about himself indicates that he did not consider himself equal to God in any way."—*Watchtower*[3]

Other Tips/Suggestions

- Don't get bogged down in endless discussions about the Trinity; instead, focus on Jesus being God and on salvation by grace through faith alone.
- Jehovah's Witnesses spend hours each and every week being taught that they are the only true church, so be prepared for a series of long conversations if you want to make any progress.
- Many Jehovah's Witnesses are former Protestants (Lutheran, Methodist, Baptist, etc.), so be prepared to listen to their past church experiences without judging them.

For Further Research

- www.dare2share.org/jehovahwitness
- *The 10 Most Important Things You Can Say to a Jehovah's Witness* by Ron Rhodes

CHAPTER 30

JENNA THE JEW

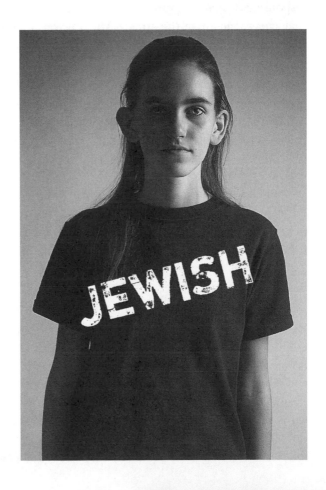

I met Jenna and her friend when I was at the mall. Standing self-consciously outside the movie theater, they were looking around for someone friendly (and older than 17) who would get them tickets to an R-rated movie. When they asked me if I would, my response got their attention. I said something like, "Are you from that synagogue down the street? And are you ditching school today to go to an R-rated movie?"

Jenna was surprised and asked me point blank, "How'd you know that?" My response was "I guess you could consider me a prophet of God. Will you let me tell you more about God?"

As we talked further, I learned that Jenna was well aware that Jesus claimed to be the Messiah, but she rejected that claim. Eventually she asked, "Since we listened to what you wanted to tell us, will you get us tickets for the movie?"

When I told her that I wouldn't, she followed up by asking, "If I'd told you I'd just accepted Jesus, would you have gotten us our tickets?" Again I told her that I wouldn't—underage entry into an R-rated movie would be no way to start a new life in Jesus!

Basic Description

Jenna was raised in a strict, religious household where Judaism and "real life" go hand in hand. All her life she has gone with her family to the Jewish temple, and at age 13 she went through the Jewish Bat Mitzvah, a ceremony that recognized her as an adult and where she pledged to uphold the Jewish law.

Jenna knows the Old Testament well and believes that one earns salvation by keeping the law. She also expects a Savior called the Messiah to come and liberate the Jewish people. She is aware that Jesus claimed to be Messiah, but rejects that claim.

Common Misconceptions
- Jenna hates all Christians.
- Jenna is rich and her parents buy and sell diamonds in New York.
- Jenna worships a different God than Christians do.

Three Fascinating Facts
- The Jewish religion started over 4,000 years ago.
- The majority of Jews do not strictly follow traditional Judaism.
- Early Christianity was considered an offshoot of Judaism by the Roman Empire.

Things We Probably Agree On
- Jenna believes in and worships the same God we believe in and worship.
- Jenna believes that Jesus existed.
- Jenna believes in the same Old Testament that we do.

Things We Probably Disagree On
- Jenna rejects the claims of Jesus as Messiah, whereas the Bible teaches Jesus proved He is the Messiah by coming back from the dead (Matthew 28:2-7).
- Jenna believes the prophecies about the Messiah weren't about Jesus, whereas the Bible teaches that Jesus was the fulfillment of the Old Testament prophecies about the coming Messiah (Luke 24:27).
- Jenna believes in salvation by keeping the Law, whereas the Bible teaches that the Law was designed to help them see their need for salvation by grace through faith (Galatians 3:10-14).

Suggested Conversation Starters
- Do you follow Judaism because of your choice, or because it is your family tradition?
- Have you ever considered the possibility that Jesus really is the Messiah? Why or why not?
- Since you believe that entrance into heaven is dependent on keeping the Law, how well have you obeyed the Ten Commandments? (Check out "The Hammer and the Healer" in chapter 11.)

A Compliment to Use
- Judaism is a religion that I've always respected. Every time I read the Old Testament I am reminded of what a great, powerful, and impacting religion Judaism was and is. Jesus Himself was Jewish and thoroughly familiar with their tradition and often quoted the law and prophets from memory.

Interesting Quotes
- "If we were forced to choose just one, there would be no way to deny that Judaism is the most important intellectual development in human history."—David Gelernter, Yale University Professor[1]
- "The wise man, even when he holds his tongue, says more than the fool when he speaks."—Jewish saying

Other Tips/Suggestions
- Remember that a Jew's religion is intricately tied to his or her family, so respect that fact when you are discussing Judaism—if you insult the religion, you insult the family.

- Don't try to show that Jesus is the Messiah from the New Testament. Use the Old Testament, but don't call it the "Old Testament." Instead, refer to it as the Hebrew Scriptures.
- Affirm and reaffirm your belief in the oneness of God (Deuteronomy 6:4), but never ever call Him "Jehovah." To the Jew this is a mispronunciation of God's sacred name and will most likely shut all future doors of opportunity for you.

For Further Research
- www.dare2share.org/jews
- *Witnessing to Jews: Practical Ways to Relate the Love of Jesus* by Moishe Rosen and Ceil Rosen

CHAPTER 31

MARTY THE MORMON

I was on a walk with my wife and my little wiener dog "Shadow" when I met Marty and friend. They were both standing in the pathway that we were on. This collision course was divine. They started the conversation by saying, "Nice dog, mister." Pretty soon we were chatting about the gospel. While Marty assured me that they were just as Christian as my wife and I were, I began to point out some major differences. As examples, I said that Mormons believe we can become gods and rule our own celestial planet someday, and the Christian church was fully corrupted and that the Mormon church was the one true church.

One of the questions I asked Marty up-front was if we could limit our conversation to the Bible, since we both believed in the Bible but differed on whether or not the Book of Mormon was the inspired Word of God. He agreed. While my wife waited patiently and prayed and Shadow wagged her tail, I went to verse after verse and showed them that there was only one God and that salvation was by faith alone, not by good deeds.

To be honest I didn't expect Marty to come to Christ on the spot (and he didn't). Marty had been raised in a Mormon family. His beliefs were deeply ingrained into his mind and soul. To leave the Mormon church meant that his family would turn their backs on him completely. My goal was to create a shadow of a doubt by presenting some indisputable scriptures in a loving way. My prayer is that I will see Marty in heaven someday, that the seeds of doubts that were sown that day grow to the garden of true salvation in his heart!

Basic Description
The official name of the Mormon church today is the Church of Jesus Christ of Latter-day Saints (LDS). Joseph Smith founded it at

the age of 24 in the state of New York on April 6, 1830. Smith claimed he was praying in a wooded grove when an angel revealed to him an additional scripture. He claimed that the text, known as the Book of Mormon, documents the ministry of Jesus Christ in the Americas after His death and resurrection 2,000 years ago in Jerusalem. Mormons believe that after the 12 apostles who founded the Christian faith died, the church fell into apostasy until Smith's vision restored the "true church."

The official LDS Web site lists the December 31, 2004, worldwide church membership at 12,275,822. At the beginning of 2005, there were approximately 5,599,000 LDS members in the United States and approximately 6,677,000 members outside of the USA.[1] Most of those outside of the USA are in Latin American countries. Several sources (including *Newsweek* and the BBC) cite Mormonism as one of the fastest-growing religions in the world.

Common Misconceptions

- Marty can marry at age 15 or 16.
- Marty and all Mormon young men wear ties and nametags and ride bikes.
- Marty can't date or dance, and his sisters can't wear makeup.

Three Fascinating Facts

- Mormonism is the most influential world religion actually founded in America.
- Mormon missionaries are allowed only two phone calls a year: Christmas and Mother's Day.
- Mormon high school students start every school day at six A.M. for seminary training where they learn the church's teaching.

Things We Probably Agree On
- Mormons believe there is a God.
- Mormons believe that Jesus Christ is a real person.
- Mormons believe the Bible is God's Word.

Things We Probably Disagree On
- Mormons believe the Book of Mormon is inspired by God (they call it "another testament of Jesus Christ"), whereas the Bible says that it shouldn't be added to or taken away from (Revelation 22:18-19).
- Mormons believe getting into heaven is through a combination of grace through faith and works, whereas the Bible says that going to heaven is by faith alone (Ephesians 2:8-9).
- Mormons believe that God was once just a man and that we too can become gods someday, whereas the Bible says there is only one true God (Isaiah 45:5).

Suggested Conversation Starters
- Why do you think that the LDS church calls itself "Christian"?
- Why do you believe the Book of Mormon is "another testament of Jesus Christ"?
- How can a person know for sure that he or she is going to heaven?

A Compliment to Use
- Mormons are among the nicest, most sincere, and hardest-working people I know.

Interesting Quotes

- "I told the brethren that *The Book of Mormon* was the most correct of any book on earth, and the keystone of our religion, and a man would get nearer to God by abiding by its precepts, than by any other book."—Joseph Smith, *History of the Church*[2]

- "There is not a man or woman, who violates the covenants made with their God, that will not be required to pay the debt. The blood of Christ will never wipe that out, your own blood must atone for it."—Brigham Young, *Journal of Discourses*[3]

Other Tips/Suggestions

- Many Mormons are not aware of the church's official doctrine, so many of the above-mentioned facts might come as a surprise to them. If this happens, don't get distracted with trying to prove you are right unless you believe it will help get that person closer to trusting Christ.

- Mormons use words and phrases that sound biblically true (Jesus Christ, Son of God, salvation by faith, etc.) but actually mean something entirely different. Because of this, it is critical that you make sure you mean the same thing. For instance, if they say, "I am trusting in Christ for my salvation," you can ask these questions:

  "What do you mean by 'salvation'?"
  "How do you define 'Jesus'?"
  "Are you trusting in Christ alone for your salvation?"

- Remember that your ultimate weapons are prayer, your testimony, and the gospel message. Your goal is not to win an argument, but to win a person! Pray for him or her as you share the gospel, and also ask God to give you wisdom, because only the Holy Spirit can convict people of sin and convert them to Christ.

For Further Research
- www.dare2share.org/mormons
- *The 10 Most Important Things You Can Say to a Mormon* by Ron Rhodes

CHAPTER 32

MO THE MUSLIM

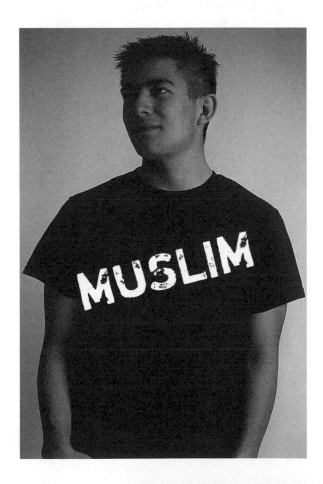

I was in downtown Denver on a date with my soon-to-be-wife when I saw a large group of men, women, and children in a park having a barbecue. At first I thought it was a church group. I asked a young man who was getting something out of his car what was going on. He told me that it was a Muslim celebration. We began to talk and as we did, we were soon in a conversation about Jesus.

Mo explained to me that Jesus was an esteemed prophet in Islam (the term for the Muslim religion) and that they had a high view of Jesus. So I began to probe a little deeper with questions like, "If Jesus was just a prophet, then why did He claim to be equal with God the Father in John 10:28-30?" or "Jesus said in John 14:6, 'I am the way and the truth and the life. No one comes to the Father except through me.' How could Jesus just be a prophet if He claimed to be the only way to heaven?"

As we talked, it became clear that he hadn't thought through the subject much. Although the conversation never morphed into an argument, it was uncomfortable for a few minutes. My prayer for Mo is that those moments of discomfort lead to his reconsidering Jesus for who He really was and is—God in the flesh!

Basic Description

Mo the Muslim follows the religion called Islam. Islam was founded in A.D. 610 by a man named Muhammad. During Muhammad's time, his people worshipped many gods, and according to Islamic history, Muhammad had a vision from a being he perceived to be an angel who said, "There is only one God, and his name is Allah. Worship him."

As a Muslim, Mo is required to accept seven fundamental tenets of Islam. Mo believes in the following:

1. God (named Allah)
2. God's angelic servants and enemies (angels and demons)
3. God's word (called the Qur'an and often referred to as the Koran, which Muslims believe was dictated to Muhammad by the angel Gabriel. They also believe that the first five books of the Bible and the Psalms are God's word as well)
4. God's prophets (Muhammad being the greatest one)
5. God's judgment (a "Last Day" for all mankind)
6. God's justice (Allah will judge each person's life on the last day based on good deeds vs. bad deeds)
7. God's resurrection (Allah will raise the dead)

If Mo wants to earn salvation, he must perform the five pillars of the Islamic faith:

1. Confess his faith by saying that Allah is the only God and Muhammad is his prophet
2. Pray five times a day: before sunrise, at midmorning, noon, midafternoon, and after sunset
3. Give voluntary contributions of money (around 2 to 3 percent of his wealth)
4. Fast during the Islamic holy season of Ramadan (a one-month period when Muslims don't eat anything from sunrise to sunset)
5. Make a pilgrimage to Mecca. (Every Muslim who is financially able is supposed to travel to the place where Islam was founded at least once in his or her lifetime)

Common Misconceptions
- Mo is a terrorist.
- Mo worships the same God as Christians.
- Mo can't be caucasion, aka "white."

Three Fascinating Facts
- The word "Islam" actually means "submission to God." Therefore, a Muslim is one who strives to submit to God.
- Islam is the world's second-largest religion with a following of over one billion people called Muslims.
- Muslims neither worship Muhammad nor pray through him. Muslims solely worship the unseen and omniscient creator, Allah.

Things We Probably Agree On
- Muslims believe that there is one God.
- Muslims believe that Jesus existed and should be respected.
- Muslims believe that there will be a final judgment day.

Things We Probably Disagree On
- Muslims don't believe Jesus was crucified (or even killed for that matter), whereas the Bible teaches He was crucified on a cross in a place called Golgotha (John 19:16-18).
- Muslims believe that salvation is available through works, whereas the Bible teaches salvation by grace through faith alone, totally apart from works (Ephesians 2:8-9).
- Muslims believe that Islam is the one true religion, whereas the Bible teaches that salvation is not found in following a religion, but through a relationship with Jesus Christ (John 14:6; Acts 4:12).

Suggested Conversation Starters
- What led you to follow the Islamic faith?
- If I could tell you how to know for sure you will go to heaven, would you be willing to listen?
- Jesus and Islam both claim to be the only path to God, so how should a person decide which one is right?

A Compliment to Use
- Muslims sure are committed to prayer! It's amazing how everyone in your religion is expected to pray five times a day!

Interesting Quotes
- "In blasphemy indeed are those that say that Allah is Christ the son of Mary."—Qur'an[1]
- "Already more than a billion-people strong, Islam is the world's fastest-growing religion."—ABC News[2]

Other Tips/Suggestions
- Ask what they have been taught about Christianity and specifically Jesus.
- Invite them into your home and reflect genuine interest in their beliefs. Be sure and give them time to explain Islam to you.
- Emphasize the claims that Jesus made about being God and the only way to heaven.
- Highlight the assurance of salvation that Christians have because of grace as opposed to works.

For Further Research
- www.dare2share.org/muslims
- *Reasoning from the Scriptures with Muslims* by Ron Rhodes

CHAPTER 33

NICOLE THE NEW AGER

My wife introduced me to Nicole. She was young, pretty, and full-on New Age in her beliefs. She had crystals, practiced meditation, did Yoga—the whole bit. When my wife and I first started talking to her about Jesus she was very open-minded. After all, being open-minded is one of the unofficial tenets of New Age thought. It didn't take very long before she understood that the spiritual fulfillment she had been looking for in the New Age movement could only be found in Jesus. Not only did she come to Christ, she came to church with us. Pretty soon she began to share Jesus with those around her with a passion. It was awesome to see somebody who had been so steeped in New Age beliefs come to Christ in such a powerful way.

Basic Description
New Age is actually not a new group. One of the core beliefs of the New Age movement is that people have a "divine spark" inside them—that we all have the potential to achieve god-like status. Over 4,000 years ago, Satan lied to Adam and Eve and told them they could be like God, and he's been repeating that lie in different forms ever since. As skeptic James Randi once said, "The New Age? It's just the old age stuck in a microwave oven for 15 seconds."[1]

New Agers also do not believe in God as a person; rather, they feel God is a term for an impersonal force, energy, or consciousness. They are into spirit contact and believe that humanity is evolving toward a "new age" of peaceful prosperity. As far as the afterlife, New Agers are similar to Wiccans in that they believe in karma and reincarnation, which is the conviction that "what goes around comes around," and that our souls are eternal and go through a series of "incarnations" (i.e., enter into flesh) as they evolve. Some New Agers may even accept the reality of some kind of heaven where everybody is welcome.

Common Misconceptions
- Each New Ager holds the same beliefs as every other New Ager.
- New Agers are constantly changing what they believe.
- New Agers have a good understanding of Christianity.

Three Fascinating Facts
- New Agers have teachers called "Metaphysical Ministers."
- New Agers believe that "God" is a combination of everyone and everything in their spiritual interconnectedness.
- Many New Age beliefs come from an attempt to merge Eastern religions (Hinduism, Buddhism, etc.) with a Western lifestyle (materialism, success, etc.).

Things We Probably Agree On
- New Agers believe that there is some truth in the Bible.
- New Agers believe that Jesus Christ existed and was a powerful, enlightened being.
- New Agers believe in an eternal soul and some kind of afterlife.

Things We Probably Disagree On
- New Agers believe in reincarnation, whereas the Bible teaches that people only die once (Hebrews 9:27).
- New Agers do not believe in the biblical concept of sin or the need for forgiveness from sin, whereas the Bible affirms that everyone on earth is sinful and needs to be forgiven (Romans 3:23).

- New Agers do not believe in a judgment day where those who trusted Christ will receive rewards and enter heaven and those who rejected Christ will be sentenced to hell, whereas the Bible teaches that this day is real (Revelation 20:11-15).

Suggested Conversation Starters
- What do you believe about Jesus Christ?
- Do you think that a person's spiritual beliefs should be a total leap of faith, or should they have some level of evidence for being true?
- What if your belief system is wrong?

A Compliment to Use
- I really appreciate that you have a spiritual view of all of life and nature. That's something we have in common!

Interesting Quotes
- "The theory of reincarnation *is* recorded in the Bible."—Shirley MacLain, New Age celebrity spokesperson[2]
- "Reincarnation is like show business, you just keep on doing it until you get it right."—Shirley MacLain[3]

Other Tips/Suggestions
- Don't expect every New Ager to believe the same thing, so make sure you let your New Age friend clearly express his or her views.
- Clearly define your terms. New Agers use a lot of words that are similar to Christianity but have completely different meanings, such as "Christ consciousness" and "God."

- Try to establish some kind of common ground with New Agers through conversation. Some examples of this could be the search for purpose and value, the reality of the afterlife, and the belief that Jesus Christ existed.
- When appropriate, point out the weaknesses in the New Age worldview, as this may create an interest in Christianity. Some of the weaknesses include:
    1. The denial of sin . . . how do you explain evil?
    2. An impersonal god . . . if God is a combination of the spiritual connectedness of everyone, how can personal beings make up an impersonal force?
    3. Lack of evidence . . . where's the proof for reincarnation?

For Further Research
- www.dare2share.org/newagers
- *Confronting the New Age* by Douglas Groothuis

CHAPTER 34

RYAN
THE RELIGIOUS

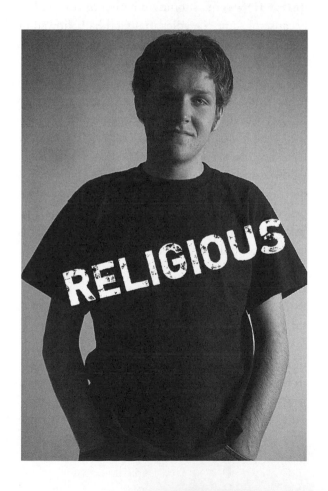

Ryan was raised in a church that tended to preach a message that heaven could be achieved through good deeds rather than received by faith in Christ alone. One day Ryan was helping me with a building project and we got into a lengthy conversation about God and justice. He was questioning whether or not God was just and fair because of some tragedies that God had allowed in the world.

I shared with Ryan that it was the justice of God that sent Jesus to the cross. That captured his attention. He always thought that it was the love of God that propelled Jesus to die for the sins of mankind. I assured him that it was both the love and the justice of God. On that hot day working outside in the blazing Colorado sun, I explained that because God was perfect and demanded perfection, it took a perfect sacrifice (Jesus) to pay for the sins of fallen humanity. Although Ryan didn't trust in Christ as his Savior on the spot, we have had several conversations since. I'm still praying for Ryan to understand that it's not his good deeds that will get him to heaven, but faith in Jesus for the act of justice and love He committed on the cross for us!

Basic Description

Ryan claims to be a Christian. But his brand of Christianity is mere religion and not a relationship with Jesus. His group goes by many names, but they have one thing in common: They are merely religious—meaning they are trying to get to heaven through a combination of faith and works. Ryan recognizes that Jesus died for his sins, but he feels he must also do good deeds in order to earn the right to go to heaven. These deeds would include (but are not limited to) things like baptism, going to church, helping the needy, and reading the Bible.

Ryan is not trusting in Christ alone for his salvation, which is why he feels it is necessary to rack up a list of spiritual accomplishments for judgment day.

Common Misconceptions
- Ryan is angry, self-righteous, and judgmental.
- Ryan knows a lot about the Bible.
- Ryan is a true Christian just because he goes to church.

Three Fascinating Facts
- The word "religion" originally meant "to bind back"—i.e., "bind" oneself back to God through good deeds.
- A Gallup Poll released in November 2003, found that 6 out of 10 Americans said that religion was "very important" in their lives.[1]
- A Google search for "religious" brings over 200 million results!

Things We Probably Agree On
- Religious people who go to church generally believe in God and Jesus.
- Religious people tend to be interested in spiritual things.
- Religious people usually believe the Bible is the Word of God.

Things We Probably Disagree On
- Ryan believes that good works are necessary for entrance into heaven, whereas the Bible teaches that the gift of eternal life is by grace through faith alone (Ephesians 2:8-9).

- Ryan believes he can earn God's favor by performing good deeds, whereas the Bible teaches that our "good deeds" are like filthy rags in God's sight (Isaiah 64:6).
- Ryan believes that the Bible is God's Word but shouldn't be taken too literally, whereas the Bible teaches that every word of it is inspired by God and should all be taken seriously (2 Timothy 3:16).

Suggested Conversation Starters
- If you stood before God and He asked you why He should let you into heaven, what would you say?
- If good works are necessary for salvation, how many do you have to do? What if you don't do enough?
- Which parts of the Bible do you think should be taken literally and which ones shouldn't, and how do you tell the difference?

A Compliment to Use
- Some of the greatest achievements of mankind, whether in the world of sciences, arts, or humanitarian service, have been done by religiously devoted individuals.

Interesting Quotes
- "But those who depend on the law to make them right with God are under his curse, for the Scriptures say, 'All who rely on observing the law are under a curse, for it is written: "Cursed is everyone who does not continue to do everything written in the Book of the Law." ' "—Galatians 3:9-10

- "Then the Lord said to him, 'Now then, you Pharisees clean the outside of the cup and dish, but inside you are full of greed and wickedness.' "—Luke 11:39

Other Tips/Suggestions

- Focus on the inconsistency of a works-based approach to getting into heaven—what is the standard for a "good" work? What if you did it with the wrong motive—does it still count? How many good works are necessary for salvation?
- Religious people have a degree of doubt about their salvation, so try and bring up the true believer's assurance of salvation.
- Ask them to show you where the Bible teaches a person can be saved from hell and enter heaven through their good works.

For Further Research

- www.dare2share.org/religious
- *The Grace Awakening* by Chuck Swindoll

SID THE SATANIST

I met Sid at the mall. Since I went to a Christian school during my high school years, I had to go out to "create" relationships with teenagers who would hang out at the mall week after week. It was there where I met Sid, a self-proclaimed Satanist.

It surprised me to know that Sid knew the Bible very well. He could quote large passages from memory. Every time I saw Sid we would talk. While he was cemented deeply into his belief system, he was very open to discuss and debate the issues of spirituality with me in a cordial way.

One night I walked into a Denny's and heard Sid yell out to me. He was sitting in the smoking section of Denny's puffing away with all of his Satanic buddies. He called me over and I came. He made me sit down and in his words give his friends "the speech." I was surprised that Sid wanted me to share the gospel with his friends, but I gladly obliged. For the next few minutes I shared the gospel with the five or six who were tucked in the big booth with Sid. Afterward while everybody was chattering about what I'd said (mostly mockingly), I leaned over to Sid and asked him if he was reconsidering his beliefs. He looked me squarely in the eyes and said, "Yes, I am."

I haven't seen Sid since. But I believe the Spirit of God was on the verge of catching him after a long chase through the abyss called Satanism. I hope to see Sid one day in heaven!

Basic Description

Sid's group is primarily made up of self-taught Satanists who for one reason or another became interested in the occult and decided to delve deeper into it. Sid practices rituals designed to bring him power and control over the world around him. These rituals include but are not limited to: incantations, Satanic ceremonies, and animal sacrifices.

Sid and his group despise anything to do with Christianity. They see believers as weak-minded people who use Jesus as a crutch. As well, Sid will tend to go for whatever brings shock value—be it clothes, music, or other cultural options that carry a Satanic theme.

Common Misconceptions
- Sid has thoroughly thought through his belief system.
- Sid believes the same things as all other Satanists.
- Sid shares the same belief system as Wiccans.

Three Fascinating Facts
- The majority of Satanists are "dabblers," meaning they are not fully immersed in it.
- One form of Satanism called "LaVey" Satanism denies the existence of Satan himself! LaVey Satanists are atheists who deny the existence of God, Satan, demons, and angels. The "Satan" that they worship is the pursuit of personal pleasure. Although most Satanists are self-styled "dabblers," the LaVey vein claims to be the true Satanic church and is an officially recognized religion in America.
- The Bible describes Satan as having the ability to disguise himself as an "angel of light" (2 Corinthians 11:14).

Things We Probably Agree On
- Sid believes that there is a God.
- Sid believes in a spiritual world complete with angels and demons.
- Sid believes that God and Satan are in a cosmic battle for the souls of mankind.

Things We Probably Disagree On

- Sid believes true power and freedom are found in Satanism, whereas the Bible teaches that following Satan enslaves a person (2 Timothy 2:25-27).
- Sid believes that occult practices are basically harmless, whereas the Bible teaches that they are incredibly dangerous and forbidden by God (Deuteronomy 18:9-11).
- Sid believes that in the end, Satan and his followers will be victorious over God, whereas the Bible teaches that God defeated Satan on the cross (Revelation 20:7-10).

Suggested Conversation Starters

- What influenced your decision to become a Satanist?
- What positive impact has Satanism had on your life?
- Have you ever considered the possibility that in the end God wins?

A Compliment to Use

- I've got to appreciate the unflinching boldness that you show in declaring yourself a Satanist in a nation where the average person describes himself as a Christian. You have a lot of courage to do that!

Interesting Quotes

- "Every religion in the world that has destroyed people is based on love."—Anton LaVey, *The Satanic Bible*[1]
- "Satan himself masquerades as an angel of light. It is not surprising, then, if his servants masquerade as servants of righteousness. Their end will be what their actions deserve."—2 Corinthians 11:14-15

Other Tips/Suggestions
- Satanists typically have a built-in hatred for Christianity, so it is key that you show the love of Jesus Christ consistently as you share Jesus. Never come across as judgmental.
- Help them understand the difference between religion/religious people and Jesus Christ. Bring up the biblical stories of how Jesus opposed religious and self-righteous people all the time.
- Try and help them see that Satanism is a trap, and true freedom is found in trusting Christ.

For Further Research
- www.dare2share.org/satanists
- *Satanism* by Bob Passantino, Dr. Alan W. Gomes

CHAPTER 36

TARA
THE TYPICAL

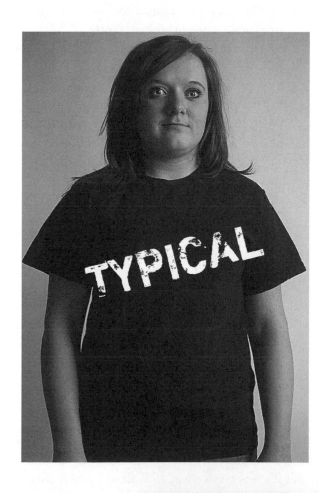

I met Tara at the mall. She was there with a friend and I just felt compelled to share Christ with her. When I asked her whether or not she was going to heaven when she died, she said that she hoped so, but didn't know for sure. I asked her if I could share with her how she could know for sure from the Bible. She said yes. Her friend listened along intently.

Over the next few minutes I shared the gospel story with Tara. She had always believed in some kind of God, but thought that if you were generally a good person (no matter which God you believed in) you would make it to heaven someday.

When she heard the gospel, that Jesus was not *a* way to heaven, but *the* way, *the* truth, and *the* life, she put her faith and trust in Christ right there in the shopping mall. She then looked at her friend with a knowing smile. She said, "I told you so." Wondering what they were talking about, I asked her what was going on. She shared with me that they had been at the mall earlier in the day and had left to go back to her house. Once there, Tara shared that something was telling her to go back to the mall. At first her friend thought she was weird, but Tara finally convinced her that something was going to happen there. That something was our conversation, and Tara knew it.

This all shows that God is working on the hearts of the Taras out there who believe what the typical person believes. God is preparing the way for your conversation with them whether they be a stranger in the mall or a friend at your school.

Basic Description
Tara the Typical is just that—a typical combination of massive media exposure, dysfunctional family dynamics, and a basic belief that there is no one way to believe when it comes to God and

spirituality. Tara is 17 years old, comes from a broken family, and believed that the vast majority of people go to heaven because most people are basically good. If there is a hell, only really bad people like Adolph Hitler and other mass murderers go there.

Tara also felt that there are many ways to God because no one religion has the absolute truth. The bottom line is that while Tara considered herself "spiritual," by no means would she have said she was "religious." Basically, the Bible and church were irrelevant to Tara because they played no significant role in helping her meet her goals of finding significant relationships and making significant money. For Tara, God was like a cosmic Santa Claus, there to answer our prayers when we need Him.

Common Misconceptions
- Tara only cares about herself.
- Tara doesn't care about spiritual things.
- Tara would never set foot in a church building (studies show that most of the Taras out there would go if they were invited by a friend!).

Three Fascinating Facts
- The typical teenager spends about 7-10 hours per week on the Internet—primarily on myspace.com, instant messaging, playing games, and/or shopping.
- They see two or three movies a week—either on DVD or in the theaters.
- They are a part of the largest generation in American history.

Things We Probably Agree On
- Typical teens believe in a God/supreme being.

- Typical teens believe in an afterlife with a heaven and possibly a hell.
- Typical teens believe in an eternal soul.

Things We Probably Disagree On

- Typical teens do not believe in absolute truth, whereas the Bible claims to be the inspired Word of God and therefore absolute truth (2 Timothy 3:16).
- Typical teens believe in an impersonal karma (i.e., what goes around comes around—both good and bad), whereas the Bible claims that there is a living, personal God who is all-powerful and ultimately decides what goes around and comes around (Revelation 19:6).
- Typical teens do not believe that Jesus is the only way to heaven, whereas Jesus claims to be just that (John 14:6).

Suggested Conversation Starters

- Do you have any spiritual beliefs? If so, would you share them with me?
- If all religions are equally true, why do so many contradict each other?
- Have you ever considered the claim Jesus made that He is the only way to heaven?

Interesting Quotes

- "I think [being a teenager] is a time in your life when you gravitate toward a somewhat dark realism, and you want people to stop talking to you as if you were a child. You want people to give it to you straight."—Rock artist Morrissey, *Spin*[1]

- "Music is the soundtrack of a person's life—it's the soundtrack of my life."—Pop singer Shakira, *Jane*[2]
- "At this point I've found a really spiritual path, and that's helped me a great amount. I used to live in fear of death—fear just overwhelmed my life. Today, there's a lot of hope for tomorrow in me."—Max Bemis, leader of emo band Say Anything, *Entertainment Weekly*[3]

Other Tips/Suggestions

- Be sure and get a clear understanding of where they are coming from before you attempt to give them the gospel. Remember the old adage: People don't care what you know unless they know that you care.
- Remember that Tara perceives a big difference between "spiritual" and "religious," so keep the conversation centered on spirituality and avoid religious-sounding terms like "saved," "born again," and "Christian."
- Try and steer the conversation toward an evaluation of their belief system in terms of logic, consistency, and the implications if their beliefs are wrong.

For Further Research

- www.dare2share.org/typical
- *The Case for Christ: Student Edition* by Lee Strobel

CHAPTER 37

WILLOW
THE WICCAN

Willow lived in my neighborhood. Almost every month a group would arrive at her house, frequently gathering in her backyard around the light of a bonfire. While many of my neighbors despised her, I tried to wave at her every time I saw her. She knew that I was a preacher and she knew that I knew she was into Wicca.

Before I shared the gospel with her I wanted to establish a firm notion in her head that I was a nice guy. I accomplished that with smiles and waves and an occasional "how are you?" conversation. I was praying for an opportunity to lovingly bring up the gospel with her.

One winter day, my wife and I heard something rustling in the backyard. At first I thought it was some kind of wild animal, a fox or something. As I looked around I saw what it was—a ferret that had escaped its home was trying to find a place in our window well to stay warm. I put some gloves on and gently grabbed it, surprised by its tameness.

I then took the next step of going door-to-door in my neighborhood to find out whose it was. As I went to house after house, I got the sinking feeling in my stomach that maybe it was Willow's. To be honest, I hoped it wasn't. Though I was friendly to Willow from a distance, I wasn't in the mood to have a Jesus conversation at her doorstep on a cold, wintery day.

As I knocked on her door she almost immediately swung it open, startling me. She yelled in excitement that I had found her lost ferret. She was so excited and thankful that she gave me some homemade pickles. She then admitted to me that I was the only neighbor who was nice to her.

Here was my chance to share Jesus, but I blew it. I thanked her for the pickles and said good-bye, justifying to myself that the door was now open to share my faith and that I would do it at a more convenient time. That time never came because soon after, she suddenly moved out. I missed the opportunity that God had given me to share with Willow and I have regretted it ever since.

Basic Description

Most Wiccans have a deep love and respect for nature and creation, but do not recognize or even believe in God as the Creator. Wiccans believe in a god and goddess, as well as a multitude of divine entities (such as spirits) and connect with them through rituals. Wicca gives its followers power in casting spells and in controlling their lives. The majority of Wiccans practice what they call "white magic"—magic that is intended to do good.

Wiccans are strong believers in karma and reincarnation—that is, the conviction that "what goes around comes around," and that our souls are eternal and go through a series of "incarnations" (i.e., enter into flesh) as they evolve.

Common Misconceptions

- Willow and her friends are witches who howl at the moon and cast dark spells.
- Willow believes in Satan.
- Willow actively tries to convert people to her beliefs.

Three Fascinating Facts

- Wicca is also known as a "neo-pagan" religion and has been around in one form or another for thousands of years.
- The initiation training for Wiccans in a coven takes about a year to complete.

- Many Wiccans believe that the god they worship is Jehovah and/or Allah.

Things We Probably Agree On
- Wiccans believe in a supreme being.
- Wiccans believe in the spiritual world.
- Wiccans believe in life after death.

Things We Probably Disagree On
- Wiccans do not believe in sin or see a need for forgiveness, whereas the Bible affirms that everyone on earth is sinful and needs to be forgiven (Romans 3:23).
- Wiccans do not believe in heaven or hell, whereas the Bible teaches the existence of both (Matthew 3:16; Luke 12:5).
- Wiccans believe there is a "good" type of magic, whereas the Bible warns that all magic/witchcraft/sorcery is evil and a serious offense to God (Deuteronomy 18:10-12).

Suggested Conversation Starters
- Have you had any other experiences with religion or religious groups? If so, what happened?
- What do Wiccans believe about Christians?
- Have you ever considered the idea that the Creator of the universe came to visit and even die for His creation?

A Compliment to Use
- One of the things I really admire about Wicca is how it so deeply respects life and nature.

Interesting Quotes
- "Sorry I missed church, I was busy practicing witchcraft."
  —bumper sticker
- "Our only animosity toward Christianity, or toward any other religion or philosophy of life, is to the extent that its institutions have claimed to be 'the only way' and have sought to deny freedom to others and to suppress other ways of religious practice and belief."—13 Principles of Wiccan Belief[1]

Other Tips/Suggestions
- One of the biggest obstacles you will have with Wiccans is their conviction that they don't need forgiveness. Because of this, focus on how all people have broken God's perfect law by going through the Ten Commandments (see chapter 11). You can also use the "three sins a day" illustration, which goes like this: Most people think they are pretty good because they can usually think of someone worse. Would you say that a person who only messed up (lied, gossiped, lusted, etc.) three times a day would be good? Most would say "yes," but think about it—if I only sin three times a day, that's over a thousand sins a year. That means if I live to be 70, I will have broken God's laws over 70,000 times!
- Wiccans typically aren't convinced that Christians are caring/loving people, so change that perception by being Christlike in everything you do!

For Further Research
- www.dare2share.org/wiccans
- *When Someone You Love Is Wiccan: A Guide to Witchcraft and Paganism for Concerned Friends, Nervous Parents, and Curious Co-Workers* by Carl McColman

NOTES

Chapter 7

1. Dictionary.com, "segue," http://dictionary.reference.com/
   search?q=segue.

Chapter 24

1. BrainyMedia.com, "Brainy Quote," *Clarence Darrow Quotes*,
   www.brainyquotes.com/quotes/quotes/c/clarenceda103622.html.

Chapter 25

1. BrainyMedia.com, "Brainy Quote," *Timothy Jones Quotes*,
   www.brainyquotes.com/quotes/quotes/t/timothyjon176701.html.
2. BrainyMedia.com, "Brainy Quote," *Arthur C. Clarke Quotes*,
   www.brainyquotes.com/quotes/quotes/a/arthurccl161414.html.
3. ThinkExist, "Thinkexist.com," *Howard Stern Quotes*,
   http://en.thinkexist.com/quotation/i_m_sickened_by_all
   _religions-religion_has/209457.html.

Chapter 26

1. A View on Buddhism, "Buddhist Quotes and Sayings," http://
   buddhism.kalachakranet.org/resources/buddhist_quotes.html.
2. Ibid.

Chapter 27

1. Charles Darwin, *The Origin of Species* (New York: Penguin
   Group [USA] Inc., 2003), p. 263.

2. The Complete Works of Charles Darwin, *Charles Darwin Quotes*, www.darwin-literature.com/l_quotes.html.

Chapter 28
1. Katha Upanishad, *The Aquarian Theosophist* 4, no.7 (May 2004): p. 7, www.teosofia.com/Docs/vol-4-7-supplement.pdf.
2. OneLittleAngel.com, "Hinduism Upanishads Quotes," www.onelittleangel.com/wisdom/quotes/book.asp?mc=215; quote #6.

Chapter 29
1. Watchtower: Official Web site of Jehovah Witnesses, "Membership and Publishing Statistics," www.jw-media.org/people/statistics.htm.
2. *1939 Yearbook of Jehovah's Witnesses* (Brooklyn: Watchtower Bible and Tract Society, 1939), p. 85.
3. Watchtower: Official Web site of Jehovah Witnesses, "Is God Always Superior to Jesus?" www.watchtower.org/library/ti/index.htm?article=article_06.htm.

Chapter 30
1. SimpleToRemember.com, "Judaism Online," *Jewish Quotes*, www.simpletoremember.com/vitals/quotes.htm.

Chapter 31
1. Newsroom.LDS.org, "Key Facts and Figures," www.lds.org/newsroom/page/0,15606,4034-1—-10-168,00.html.
2. Joseph Smith, *History of the Church*, Vol. 4 (Salt Lake City, Utah: 1978), p. 461. No publisher given.

3. Brigham Young, *Journal of Discourses*, Vol. 3 (Salt Lake City, Utah: 1967), p. 247. No publisher given.

Chapter 32

1. Abdullah Yusuf Ali, *The Meaning of the Holy Qur'an* (Beltsville, Md: Amana Publications, 2003), p. 251.
2. Islamic Invitation Center, "Who are the Muslims?" www.islamicinvitationcentre.com/articles/Introduction/fastest/fastest_planet.html.#Anchor-AB-38902.

Chapter 33

1. WeBlogALot, "WeBlogALot.com," www.weblogalot.com/Archive/2003/03/30/08.
2. Shirley MacLaine, *Out on a Limb* (New York: Bantam Books, 1983), p. 237.
3. Ibid., p. 235.

Chapter 34

1. Polling Report.com, "Religion," *The Gallup Poll*, May 2-4, 2004, www.pollingreport.com/religion.htm.

Chapter 35

1. Think Exist, "Thinkexist.com," *Anton LaVey Quotes*, http://en.thinkexist.com/quotes/anton_lavey.

Chapter 36

1. GroundZero Ministries, "The Center for Parent/Youth Understanding's Youth Culture E-Update," May 5, 2004, edition 58, *Pop Culture Quotes*, http://gzyouth.com//Parents/CYPU/ParentLetter58.htm.

2. GroundZero Ministries, "The Center for Parent/Youth Understanding's Youth Culture E-Update," December 15, 2005, edition 84, *Pop Culture Quotes*, http://cpyu.org/files/e-Update/CPYU%20e-Update-84.doc.
3. Ibid.

Chapter 37

1. The Internet Sacred Text Archive, "Principles of Wiccan Beliefs," www.sacred-texts.com/bos/bos056.htm.

ABOUT THE AUTHOR

Greg Stier is the founder and president of Dare 2 Share Ministries (D2S). Over the last decade, Greg has impacted the lives of hundreds of thousands of teenagers across the country through Dare 2 Share training conferences. Dare 2 Share's vision is to equip 1,000,000 Christian teens across the nation to know, live, and share and own their faith in Jesus. Greg's prayer is that God will use the ministry and these equipping events to launch a spiritual awakening through an army of youth leaders, teenagers, pastors and parents.

D2S also provides free online resources and a vast array of curriculum, books, and other training resources for students and youth leaders. For more information on Dare 2 Share training conferences or how to start an e-team (a team of students who lead the way for outreach on a youth-group level), go to www.dare2 share.org. Look for the free resource Soul Fuel and sign up to receive it online.

Other resources by Greg Stier:

- **Ministry Mutiny: A Youth Leader Fable**—An engaging parable of one man's struggle toward life-changing leadership. This catalytic, relevant look at the youth ministry culture provides a much needed wake up call for the sleeping church and an action plan for change.
- **GOSPEL Journey Adventure Kit**—Follow seven very different students on an unscripted Rocky Mountain adventure through the gospel in this reality DVD series. Designed to be used as an evangelism training tool for Christian teens and an evangelistic outreach tool for non-Christian teens, this journey unfolds with raw, real, and riveting discussions.
- **Outbreak: Creating a Contagious Youth Ministry Through Viral Evangelism**—Discover how the power of the gospel can unleash a contagious epidemic to change not only lives, but entire societies!
- **Battle Zone** Put on the indestructible armor and ready the powerful weapons provided by your Supreme Commander! Then step into battle armed with His plan to free the prisoners and make you a mighty soldier!

To contact Dare 2 Share Ministries
e-mail info@dare2share.org,
call (800) 462-8355
or write
Dare 2 Share Ministries,
PO Box 745323,
Arvada, CO 80006-5323

FOCUS ON THE FAMILY®

teen outreach

At Focus on the Family, we work to help you really get to know Jesus and equip you to change your world for Him.

We realize the struggles you face are different from your parents' or your little brother's, so we've developed a lot of resources specifically to help you live boldly for Christ, no matter what's happening in your life.

Besides teen events and a live call-in show, we have Web sites, magazines, booklets, devotionals, and novels . . . all dealing with the stuff you care about. For a detailed listing of the latest resources, log on to our Web site at **www.go.family.org/teens.**

Breakaway®
Teen guys
breakawaymag.com

Focus on the Family Magazines

We know you want to stay up-to-date on the latest in your world—but it's hard to find information on relationships, entertainment, trends, and teen issues that doesn't drag you down. It's even harder to find magazines that deliver what you want and need from a Christ-honoring perspective.

That's why we created *Breakaway* (for teen guys), *Brio* (for teen girls 13 to 15), and *Brio & Beyond* (for girls ages 16 and up). So, don't be left out — sign up today!

Brio®
Teen girls 13 to 15
briomag.com

Brio & Beyond®
Teen girls 13 to 15
briomag.com

Phone toll free: (800) A-FAMILY (232-6459)
In Canada: (800) 232-6459

More Great Resources
from Focus on the Family®

TRIBE: A WARRIOR'S CALLING
By Jeremy V. Jones & Greg Asimakoupoulos
(Introduction by Michael Ross)

Face it: You're bombarded with hundreds of conflicting messages every day. What's more, friends—even strangers—attempt to pull you in a dozen different directions. In this world of high-tech toys and low-minded values, which voices should you tune in? This daily devotional will challenge you to trust in Jesus as never before. – Trade copy

STAND
Core Truths You Must Know for an Unshakable Faith
By: Alex McFarland

With humor and stories gleaned from decades of working with youth, McFarland encourages teens to build a foundation of faith that will stabilize their lives and help them take a stand for Christ. Key concepts of biblical Christianity are presented in an easy-to-understand style: biblical inspiration, the Virgin Birth, the deity of Christ, the Atonement, and the Resurrection and return of Christ. – Trade copy

WANT MORE? JOY
By Jeanette Hanscome

Teen girls need assurance that God wants them to have more—more joy, more trust, more connection with Him. With *Want More? Joy,* girls will discover the real joy that comes from God, who loves us without limit. Companion books include *Want More? Life* and *Want More? Love.* – Trade copy

FOR MORE INFORMATION

 Online:
Log on to www.family.org
In Canada, log on to www.focusonthefamily.ca.

 Phone:
Call toll free: (800) A-FAMILY
In Canada, call toll free: (800) 661-9800.

BP06XP1